Brian Eldridge

THE
SHRAPNEL
KID

A memoir of a wartime childhood, the world of work
in a Dickensian dockyard and National Service in the
Royal Army Medical Corps

Mereo Books

2nd Floor, 6-8 Dyer Street, Cirencester, Gloucestershire, GL7 2PF
An imprint of Memoirs Books. www.mereobooks.com
and www.memoirsbooks.co.uk

The Shrapnel Kid
ISBN: 978-1-86151-977-1

First published in Great Britain in 2021
by Mereo Books, an imprint of Memoirs Books.

Copyright ©2021

Brian Eldridge has asserted his right under the Copyright Designs and Patents
Act 1988 to be identified as the author of this work.

The address for Memoirs Books can be
found at www.mereobooks.com

Mereo Books Ltd. Reg. No. 12157152

Typeset in 11/15pt Century Schoolbook
by Wiltshire Associates.
Printed and bound in Great Britain

Preface

This little autobiography relating to my life up to the end of my National Service at the age of twenty years has been written from memory, with no research except in explanation of the V1 and V2 flying bombs. If any readers find fault with my comments and observations I accept that, but it is told as I remember it, picturing and interpreting the events of that time.

I wanted to chronicle this period for my daughters Gemma and Bronwen, my grandchildren Ruby, Ethan and Summer and my wife Joy, as they have no knowledge of this era of my life, only post National Service. This book will I hope fill in the gap with pleasant memories of me and enable them to understand the love I have for them.

Contents

1   A wartime childhood 1

2   Schooldays 42

3   Off to work 53

4   My mother...................................... 101

5   Farewell to the docks 103

6   A job in the lab 109

7   Called up 128

8   Royal Army Medical College 154

9   The toss of a coin 162

10 Winding down towards demob 217

    Postscript 237

Chapter 1

A wartime childhood

I was born in 1935 and lived in Barking on a small estate consisting of Craven Gardens, Westminster Gardens and Waverley Gardens. It was near the Volunteer Pub; River Road led down to Barking Creek or the Creekmouth, Barking.

My first recollections are from 1939. I was one and a half years older than my brother Peter; I was four and a half years old. I remember my mother and my father waking us and quickly dressing us in our red home-made dressing gowns with red and white piping at the sleeve and front edges. Later on in the war we had silk sashes made from parachute silk and barrage balloon cords.

My brother had a white toy Scottie dog and I had a black one (the whisky emblem). I remember the rising and falling wail of the siren, when we were carried in their arms out into the garden and down into the Anderson shelter. I vaguely remember our garden without the shelter and also with it, but I do not remember it being constructed. The shelter was of corrugated iron and consisted of two 'J' shaped sections bolted together at the top and then bolted to two end sections, one end section having a square hole for the doorway. A hole had to be dug, four feet deep and seven by six feet in area. When the sections were placed and bolted together in position my father cemented the floor and the sides to provide a concrete ledge surround. He fitted hammocks to securing bolts. There were blankets and cushions, and many candles stood in bottles around the concrete ledge.

My father, with the help of my uncles, found many old railway sleepers behind the Dicky Birds custard factory, opposite the fire station, close to the Barking bypass and River Roding. They were part of the railway track for mobile cranes by the Barking quay many years ago.

The sleepers were carried two at a time on a wheelbarrow. Three shelters were covered using six sleepers for each one and four were laid on top with one on each side. The shelter was then covered in earth and then by a sheet or tarpaulin, also discovered by the railway track. Some had eyelets to secure ropes as used to cover cargo hatches on the barges. The whole shelter was decorated with pots of flowers. The opening to the shelter was covered with a thick wooden door that was hingeless but had a handle on the inside to close after you. Every household decorated their shelter in a different way. Some had a primus stove for making tea and heating tinned food.

When my brother and I were carried to the shelter we were put into the hammocks and covered with blankets. My parents sat on a couple of stools with cushions and I lay awake clutching my Scottie. We lay in our hammocks huddled up, my brother usually asleep or in my mother's arms, and it felt safe. I do not recall too much anxiety but an occasional worry as I watched my parents staring up at the corrugated roof, not saying much, but there was an occasional flinch when an explosion was loud and a bit close for comfort.

After a while the all-clear siren went, a continuous note with no undulations. My parents grabbed us out of the hammocks and carried us back to bed. Nothing had happened, it had been quiet, no bombs, no ack ack (anti aircraft guns). This happened a couple of times a night. The Luftwaffe was bombing airfields. It was not until September 1940 that the Luftwaffe started to bomb the docks and most of London.

By the time I was about six my parents no longer grabbed my brother or me when the siren went. We were able to run quick enough to get to the shelter before them. We sometimes lingered a little to look up at the sky. To us it was exciting seeing the searchlights crisscrossing the sky and reflecting off barrage balloons. However we were firmly ushered into the shelter by mother.

On one occasion it rained all night. This was good news, because although bombings were now infrequent anyway, this sort of weather usually meant a peaceful night. The following morning at breakfast the rain had stopped, and we had almost finished our porridge oats and toast when the siren went. My father was about to go to work at Beckton gasworks. 'OK boys, down the dugout' he said. Grabbing a piece of toast, I followed my brother through the lean-to and into the garden at a run. My father and mother were close behind. They did not hear the splashes and shouts from my brother and me: the shelter was full of water. 'Bugger it!' said my father. 'George!' my mother reprimanded him as they came in almost on top of us. It would not have been so bad, but it was cold and full of drowned spiders and earwigs. The hammocks were clear of water. My parents stripped our clothes off, dried us with one blanket and wrapped us in another and put us in our hammocks where we were quite snug. Our parents, however, were up to their thighs in water and shivering. There we stayed for about twenty minutes before the all-clear sounded. Obviously a false alarm.

The following day my father, after work, built a step guard

and runway gutters so that the rain would not flow into the shelter again. It took us all evening to bail out the water and a paraffin heater dried it out eventually.

It was during this period that my father brought home two tin hats for my brother and me. They fitted, and we were very proud of them. I have since wondered whether they were specially made for us or were standard fitting for small-headed soldiers or air raid wardens.

Some weekends, relatives would visit. We lived in Craven Gardens. My Uncle Ted and Aunt Rose and further along another aunt and uncle, Bob and Elsie, with my grandmother, Anne Styles, lived five minutes away in Westminster Gardens. My Uncle Snowie and Aunt Ethel lived there too, but closer to the Barking bypass with my Uncle Fred and Aunt Lucy who lived upstairs. They were related on my mother's side. My father's side of the family lived in Dagenham. They came round for tea or dinner usually on Sundays and often finished up in the shelters. We also visited them on alternate weekends. This I enjoyed because my aunts and uncles brought things to eat and chatted and laughed. All crowded into one shelter.

I must clarify, not all the relatives came on the same day. This would have been rather sardine-like. After our dinner, if not in the shelter they would play cards and eat winkles in vinegar, picking out the winkles with a pin. My brother and I and our cousins enjoyed soaking up the winkle vinegar with a slice of bread. The grown-ups would usually be playing pontoon or 'Tuppenny-Ha'penny' using farthings kept in an old tin as 'chips'.

This situation continued until 1941 when night-time visits to the shelter seemed to stop. Daytime bombings were sporadic and less frequent.

At the beginning of the raids we had an Alsatian bitch named Judy. We loved her but when the air raids started, we had to get rid of her because she became very nervous. The police came one day and took her away. My father said she would be trained to work for the police or the army and that she would be all right. I often dreamt of Judy and would occasionally, according to my mother, call out her name in my sleep.

Although the air raids were less frequent, we had a Morrison shelter delivered. This was a steel cage supported by angle iron struts at each corner, about three feet high, the size basically was that of a double bed. Morrison shelters were put in bedrooms, replacing the bed. The bed was made up inside this shelter. This meant that when the sirens went at night you could stay in the house in bed. If the house got hit you were safe at least from falling masonry. They saved many lives during the V1 (Doodlebug) and V2 period of the war.

I remember during the period before the V1 and V2 that we lived downstairs. Upstairs in our house there lived another couple. They had been bombed out of their home and my father let them have the upstairs. They had three rooms, but we only saw them when the sirens went.

As the air raids became less frequent, we were allowed to play in the streets again. The Spitfire and Hurricane fighter planes were getting the upper hand. Barrage balloons were a common sight. After the war when they were taken away the sky seemed unnaturally bare.

One fine day my father took me on his bike on the crossbar into town to buy some leather and some 'segs' to repair our shoes. 'Segs' were spiked metal plates in the shape of a crescent, of various sizes and not usually more than an inch long. They were hammered onto the sole of the shoe either heel or toe.

On the road into town we heard a loud droning getting louder. Only then did we hear the sirens. After about two minutes the sky was full, it seemed, of aircraft. They were so low I could even make out the pilots in the cockpits. My father said loudly, 'Bugger me, Heinkels and Junkers'. This was the first time I had heard my father swear, although I had heard it many times from my Uncle Snowie.

My father 'kerbed' the bike and grabbed me from the crossbar, then ran into the first house, out the back and into the shelter. Most if not all doors during this time were kept open so that people could find shelter. The bombers passed over us, heading towards the docks.

During the heaviest periods of bombings, my brother and I were evacuated to High Wycombe. This lasted for two weeks. My brother and I hated it and my mother could not bear being without us. Other children from Craven Gardens and neighbouring streets also returned home about the same time for the same reasons.

A new school with different people and different 'parents' was quite depressing. I often wondered how those that were sent far afield to the country and abroad felt. Some I now know had a terrible time, whilst others enjoyed their long 'holiday'. Some of course never returned. Those that were evacuated from the city and the dock areas might never have survived if they had stayed.

Sirens used to go off throughout the day. If we were playing some distance down the end of the street from our house we could run into any house and down the shelter, but usually we had time to get home. Front doors were always open. Adults would look down the street after an air raid warning to see if anyone, a child in particular, was about.

Most weekends in the street we would be playing 'Tippy-cat', which is played in the street using the pavement kerb as a base. A two-foot square was chalked from the kerb into the street. The 'Tippy-cat' gear consisted of a stick about two feet long, which was the bat or 'tippy', and the 'cat', which is a piece of wood about four inches long, sharpened almost to a point at both ends. There were two teams of equal number if possible; the number in each team did not matter, however. One side was fielding, the other batting. The first member of the batting side placed the 'cat' overhanging the kerb in the box area. The 'cat' was then hit with a downward stroke so that it would spin away, usually in the air. If it went into the box however, you were out. If struck well into the air and the 'cat' was caught by a fielder you were also out. If neither of these disasters took place then the batsman had three goes at striking the 'cat' on one of the pointed ends so that it spun into the air, whereby the batter struck it as far away as possible, trying to avoid once again being caught.

You then retreated back to the chalked box. A fielder would then throw the 'cat' to try and get it into the box, in which case you were out. The batsman would defend the box with the 'tippy' striking at the 'cat' and avoiding again being caught. The distance away from the box, whether struck away or where the throw reached, was measured. The measure was the 'tippy', and the number of runs equalled the number of tippy lengths. The 'cat', when hit, would fizz through the air and sometimes through a window.

We played cricket, using lampposts as the wicket. Cigarette cards were won or lost as they were flicked against a fence. A card covering another won that card. Alternatively cards were placed upright against the fence and you claimed those you knocked down by flicking a card against them.

Marbles were played in the gutter. If you hit another player's marble as you travelled along the street you claimed that marble, avoiding of course losing your marbles down a drain hole.

'High Jimmy Knacker' was a bruising game, not allowed for girls. Two teams were picked, the heavier the better. One team went to the fence and formed a 'caterpillar' by locking onto the boy in front, head between his legs and grasping him around the thighs from behind. The opposing side would then, one by one, run up to the tail end of the caterpillar and leap onto the boys' backs as far up the caterpillar chain as possible. He would then hang on and keep still, not falling off or touching the ground, or he would be disqualified and not take part.

The rest of the opposing team then did the same, one by one, leaping as high and as far up the chain as possible. When all were aboard a shout went up 'High Jimmy Knacker one two three!' This was done three times, rocking on the boys' backs and jumping up and down without letting the feet touch the ground, otherwise disqualification. Boys would sway and dig with their knees, trying to collapse the caterpillar. If the caterpillar withstood the onslaught after the third 'High Jimmy Knacker' then they had one point, otherwise it was one point to the team leapfrogging. At the end of the game there were usually a few bruises and torn clothes. Not a game that pleased our parents.

'Kingie' was another game played the length of the street, from one end of the street to the other. If you were nominated as 'it' you would tamp the ball towards the other players and when they were in range throw the ball at them. If hit they would join you and you would then pass the ball between you, advancing on the others. If the ball was thrown at you, you could either dodge it or punch it away with your fists. If the ball struck any other part of the body, you joined the attackers. Last person to survive was the winner. This was another bruising game. The ball was a tennis ball and could sometimes hurt.

Of course there were the usual games played in the streets, using home-made wooden guns, with a ratchet to make a machine-gun noise. We attacked each other hiding behind and in hedges and fences. We played hockey with all shapes of sticks and skated on metal-wheeled roller skates clamped to our shoes. Those with bikes, three and two-wheelers, also joined in. The metal wheels on the skates wore out very quickly and had to be replaced.

After an air raid we would rush out and collect shrapnel. It came in all shapes and sizes, with a smooth side and a rough, jagged side. These collections were swapped among us. The prize pieces were those with recognisable markings on them. They were usually two to four inches long and about an inch wide.

'Swopsies' as we termed the exchanges, were also carried out with cigarette cards and marbles.

Later on in the war shrapnel collecting was discouraged. We became aware how dangerous shrapnel was. We called it shrapnel but they were in fact shell fragments, shrapnel being the ball bearings and other objects discharged when a Shrapnel shell exploded, invented by a British general of that name.

One of the boys in our class lost his father to a shell fragment. One night his father was shaving in the bathroom. The siren went and the boy and his mother went to the shelter. The father decided to finish his shave. The Barking Park ack-ack (anti-aircraft gun) had opened up, and a piece from an exploded shell came through the roof, through the door of the bathroom and through the man's back.

The German bombers started to drop 'Butterfly' bombs, an anti-personnel device. They were so called because the small explosive container had rods protruding with flat wing–like metal squares at the ends. If these were touched they exploded. They were dropped I think by parachute.

Every household had a stirrup pump, a bucket of water or sand and a dustbin lid, positioned for easy access in case of incendiary bombs. If an incendiary bomb was dropped, you had to quickly grab the stirrup pump, stick the cylinder part of the pump into the bucket of water, grab the dustbin lid, holding it by the handle as a shield, and with a foot on the 'leg' outside the bucket pump, aim the pipe at the bomb and put it out with the water jet.

Gas masks were taken everywhere. They were carried in cardboard boxes with a string attachment to go round your neck or crosswise over your shoulder. Grown-ups had metal tubular containers or army issue khaki square cases. I can smell the gas masks now, a rubbery sort of smell mixed with old sweat.

Although we loathed them we had some fun shouting to each other with them on. It sounded as though you were in a deep well. Best of all was to suck air in, deeply, and blow it out quickly, causing the air to escape around the rubber sides, making a very realistic farting noise. Not popular with parents!

Small children had so called 'Mickey Mouse masks'. They looked nothing like Mickey Mouse but had a blue triangular flat floppy nosepiece. The red face part had two viewing eyepieces instead of the usual single rectangular one that we had, and the filter base was blue. This was meant to look funny to the child and make it less disturbing to put on. They frightened the life out of me, and also I think the children who had to wear them. Babies were put in a sort of tent, a giant gas mask that fitted in the pram. However not once were they ever used in earnest.

Saturday was a good day, as it was sweet ration day. We always had a Mars bar. This was cut into four and my brother and I had the end pieces because of the extra chocolate. Mum and Dad had the two very thin inner slices. We also had two pence (less than half a new penny today), as pocket money. With this money we went to the corner shop-cum-café that led onto River Road. Here we bought two ounces of pear drops, boiled sweets with a smell of amyl acetate, like nail varnish. They cost us one farthing. These were sold in a twist of paper.

My mother also made sweets by heating some of our sugar ration or some Tate and Lyle golden syrup in a saucepan with water mixed with dried milk and flour. This was heated until it was difficult to stir and then it was spooned out onto greaseproof paper and rolled into cigar-shaped lengths. These were left to harden and then chopped into one-inch lengths. Another sort of sweet we had was our bedtime treat of a Horlicks tablet.

My uncle Snowie and aunt Ethel made bread pudding, which

he called 'Clagger'. I believe it was called that because it was chewy or claggy. Ethel used to get Snowie to do the mixing. Usually he was in the garden and when called to do the mixing he would come in and mix without washing his hands. However, even with the addition of earth from his vegetable patch it still tasted great and was always a treat.

Snowie was a tough, wiry character with a large Roman nose and a heart of gold, mixed with a great sense of humour. He was nicknamed Snowie because he had a wisp of white hair that hung over his forehead, not because his surname was White. Strangely after the war it started to turn ginger and he was called 'Ginge', but not to us children – to us he was always Uncle Snowie.

He had a technique when nailing pieces of wood together that was fascinating to watch. He would have a mouthful of nails, the ends of which protruded from his lips. He would hold the wood to be nailed with the back of his hand, spit a nail into the upturned palm, catch it and turn the nail with his thumb and forefinger, and with two blows of the hammer drive the nail home.

His hands were large and calloused. He could pick up a red-hot glowing coal that had fallen from the grate and without hurry place it back on the fire. Cigarettes would be smoked down to the last quarter of an inch, sometimes with the aid of a pin, without seemingly burning his lips.

He worked on a crane that ran on rails in the London docks for the Port of London Authority. He had had previous jobs, like boxing, I believe at fair booths. That was probably the cause of his Roman nose. He also had a job as a waiter in a restaurant, but this did not last long. He apparently got the sack for tipping, accidentally I think, a bowl of soup down the front of a particularly fussy woman's blouse.

Snowie used to maintain that handkerchiefs were unhygienic. Blowing noses into handkerchiefs and then putting it plus all the mucus back into one's pocket was daft, according to him, although we were, during the war, constantly reminded 'Coughs and sneezes spread diseases, trap your germs in your handkerchief'. He used to close one nostril with his finger and blow, blasting the offending mucus out of the other nostril to wherever. He did this to us too, whenever we had a runny nose.

He had many curses. Some I still have difficulty with regarding their interpretation and origin. 'Cor' or 'Gor blimey' is a bastardisation of 'God blind me' and 'Cor lummy', God love me. 'Swipe me Gawd' is 'so help me God, but 'Blind ol' pole' I have no idea! Perhaps 'ol pole' refers to the devil.

Snowie had a brother; I think his name was Joe. We only saw him at Christmas. He would frighten us by covering his head with a busted balloon stretched over his face, making him look very ghoulish. He worked in Canning Town Market with a barrow and always brought balloons for us. He also always brought a bottle of whisky for the grown-ups, and like Snowie he would joke and make Aunt Daisy, Sylvia and Iris giggle all the time. Sylvia, or Sylvie as she was better known, always loudly protested that he was very rude.

My father had his own peculiar sense of humour too. When dressing to go out he would say, 'Right I'm ready, I've got my high-heeled skirt on, my three-speed walking stick, my clockwork orange is in my humpty-back waistcoat and I've got on my best shoes with double-breasted bootlaces. I've closed the hot and cold sliding doors, so now I'm off.'

My father came from a fairly well-to-do family and was often referred to as 'Educated George'. His family were once very well off and better educated. My upbringing therefore was a mixture of the lovable Cockney Styles family and the once well-to-do Eldridges. His father, my grandfather, who died before I was born, owned the first spring mattress-making factory under the name of James. He was always known as Mr James and not Mr Eldridge. During the First World War my grandfather was in the Royal Army Medical Corps.

My mother used to work in the factory, and that's how she met my father. However, they went bankrupt. I have no recollection of the period before bankruptcy – before I was born I think. I remember having two parrots, a couple of dogs and a car, a Lanchester, and later a 1936 Rover, but these memories are vague; perhaps I was told about them and they became a false memory. We also apparently owned a couple of houses, in Barking and in Dagenham.

The relations on my father's side consisted of two sisters, Flo and Alice. Alice was deaf from birth, a kindly lovable person who could lip read perfectly. She never married. Flo married Ed and had twin daughters at this time. My grandmother Eldridge, as I recall, was usually very strict and I did not like visiting her. We had to be on our best behaviour, and it was very boring.

My grandmother on my mother's side, a cripple, once a nurse and midwife, was previously married to a Mr Chivers, but he died.

A son from that union, Harry, was blown up by a shell in 1916 with 10th Battalion Essex Regiment at the battle of the Somme. His name is on the Thiepval Memorial, Belgium. There were also two daughters, Liz and Daisy. Liz, the elder, married a Mr Hibbert and they had one son, John, who died of tuberculosis at the age of about twenty. Aunt Lizzie after his death claimed she was still in contact with him and became very involved in spiritualism.

There was also an Uncle Joe, but I do not remember him very well. He had a son, also Joe, but I don't remember him at all. Daisy had three children: a son who joined the Air Force, Billy, who went to Canada, and Iris and Sylvie. Aunt Daisy was a little deaf and I only remember her saying 'Is the kettle on, Snowie?' or

'Any more tea in the pot Snowie?' Snowie would shout back very loudly in her ear, pretending he had not heard, 'Want a cup of tea Daisy?' which frightened the life out of her and made her giggle nervously, to which Snowie would say loudly, 'Stupid old cow'.

Snowie, we were told, was also hard of hearing, but I found out that he was not. I caught him turning around when his name was whispered by one of my aunts. He saw me and said 'Don't you ever let on son OK?' I nodded. It was his way of ignoring his wife, my Aunt Ethel, and others when he was called so that he could go about his business.

Snowie never said 'Goodbye'; he always said 'See you on the eighth of October'. This caught on with everyone. What was special about the eighth of October no one could say.

My Gran's second marriage was to Joseph Styles and they had four daughters; a fifth died at birth. They were Louise (my mother), Ethel, Nancy (Nance) and Lucy. There were two sons, Bob and Ted. My Aunt Rose was married to Ted and my Aunt Elsie married Bob. Snowie (real name George) was married to Ethel. She was always singing 'Here we are again, happy as can be, all good pals and jolly good company'. Snowie was thin and wiry, Ethel, with respect, fat. I always had a picture in my mind of Laurel and Hardy when I saw them together.

Nancy was married to Fred, who was Gene Kelly's doppelganger in my mind, although I never saw him dance. Ethel and Snowie were good dancers and later became fanatic 'Come Dancing' fans. Their son George and his partner Mollie won a foxtrot championship in the fifties. Fred was about five foot six inches tall and was a fitness and physique-conscious man. Lucy was at first married to a Mr Saddington. I don't remember him; I think they parted company. She had three daughters at this time, Barbara, June and Kay. Later she had two sons with a Mr Bunting, but this was after the war. She was quite poor and other members of the families took turns in looking after her.

Some of my street friends were also hard up – not that anyone was well off in our area. However, neighbours used to drop unwanted clothes in a bag on their doorstep, unnoticed so as not to cause embarrassment.

My mother used to make most of our clothes, as did most women during the war. Knitting was a constant occupation. My mother knitted for my brother and me Fair Isle pullovers, Balaclava helmets for the winter, caps, trousers and coats. Unfortunately she also knitted swimming trunks. We hated them because they got so heavy and soggy when wet that we couldn't keep them up.

All my aunts and uncles had coal fires but my Granny Styles, first name Anne, had a black kitchen range in the living room which kept it warm. This was where she cooked her meals, made her bread, kept the iron hot and always had a kettle on for tea. She 'blacked' the range every day. We did not have the luxury of a 'fridge', nor had any other family that I was aware of. Granny Styles became crippled during the war, and my brother and I used to collect her in her wheelchair and race her round the corner to our house at weekends. We sometimes rounded the corner on one wheel. She loved to be collected by us in preference to my mother, who used to wheel her along very sedately.

My father dug a hole in the garden close to the house, about a foot and a half deep, in which we kept an old sweet tin, about a foot high and six inches wide with a tight-fitting lid. We kept our butter, cheese ration and milk in this tin and it was quite efficient. Meat was scarce, being rationed, so my mother made potato pies or carrot casseroles that were topped with sliced potato and baked in the oven, sometimes with the addition of corned beef or spam.

Bacon and suet puddings were a favourite. These were cooked in a similar manner to our Christmas puddings. Chopped bacon was mixed with suet, flour and onion, placed in a china basin, covered with a cloth and secured with string, the ends of the cloth pulled over the basin and tied with a knot. These were placed in a copper boiler, normally used for boiling our clothes and heated by a gas ring underneath. The gas was turned on via a spigot and with lighted match one reached underneath to the gas ring, the time lapse allowing sufficient gas to be emitted to ignite with a boom, singeing fingers and eyebrows.

Clothes boiled in this copper were scrubbed clean using a washboard and lifted out of the boiler with large wooden tongs. The washboard was a corrugated sheet of glass in a wooden frame with two short legs at the base. This was held in a sink of suds and clothes, the clothes being rubbed up and down vigorously on the corrugated glass until the dirt came out, especially from shirt collars, attached or unattached. The clothes were then thoroughly rinsed and the water squeezed out with a mangle. Ours had large wooden rollers with a large screwing device on top to regulate the pressure according to the thickness of the material. The clothes were then hung out on the garden clothesline. When ironed they were folded and put away in a drawer with mothballs. Even with mothballs clothes had to be shaken out regularly, otherwise they would quickly become holed by moths.

If the weather was bad clothes were hung in front of the fire on a wooden clotheshorse. This was a common sight.

Carpet cleaning was a chore. Carpets were hung on a line in the garden and beaten with a stick or wicker carpet beater. This was, fortunately, only done about once a week. They were beaten until no more dust came from them. A choking chore!

When my mother or my aunts were going out, usually to the cinema on a Saturday, they would dress up. To compensate for the lack of stockings they would colour their legs with tea or gravy browning and then draw a black line down the back of the legs with an indelible pencil to simulate the seam. It got a bit messy during hot sweaty weather or when it rained.

One Saturday afternoon we went to the pictures with my Aunt Nance and Uncle Fred and my mother. These trips were usually family outings, especially during the latter part of the war when air raids were less frequent. Air raid warnings were flashed on the screen as the sirens could not be heard in the cinema, but most people would remain in their seats. It was probably a thriller we went to see that day, because my Uncle Fred was engrossed in the film. He managed to find a loose piece of cotton which he began to roll up into a ball. He continued to do this, not realising it was cotton from the seam of his trousers. When the film ended and the lights came on, he stood up only to find that all he had for trousers were two flaps hanging down to his ankles, showing his knobbly knees and his underpants. He realised to his horror that he had pulled the stitching out from the seam of one leg, across the crotch and down the other leg. He quickly sat down and did not get up even for the people trying to pass him on their way out. Aunt Nance went to the foyer, found the manager and acquired several pins and paper clips. She secured his trousers well enough for him to get home without too much embarrassment. To us it was hilarious.

Considering our diet, we were all pretty healthy. However boils and carbuncles were fairly common especially on the forearms and neck at collar level, for obviously sweat and dirt did not help. My mother dealt with them efficiently with boiling water and lint. With the aid of tweezers she soaked the lint in the boiling water and poured it from a kettle into a pudding basin with salt. When she could just stand the heat of the lint close to the back of her hand she would slap it onto the offending boil. This was held on until it cooled a little or we shouted that we could not stand it anymore. The process continued, with much pain from the scalding, until the boil erupted. By that time we patients had had more than enough. Finally a poultice of kaolin or mixtures of zinc or magnesium sulphate was secured with a bandage.

The cause, apart from diet, was the fact that clothes were worn for about three days before changing them. This was to conserve soap and save on gas. Washday was on Mondays only. To this day I still have sixpence-sized scars on my forearms to remind me of my mother's medical practices. After the war she became a nurse, midwife and social worker and went to New Zealand to live and work mainly with the Maoris.

Our meals were supplemented with rose hip syrup for our vitamin C, syrup of figs, concentrated orange juice and once a week, thankfully not more often, the abominable tablespoon of cod liver oil.

Knowledge of medicine was mixed with old wives' tales during the war. If you had an infected eye, a stye, you were told to rub a gold ring on it for a cure. It never worked. My Uncle Snowie, referring to a sick workmate, said when asked what was wrong with him 'E's got a cardiac heart' and could not understand what the laughter was about.

Diseases during the war were mainly tuberculosis, whooping cough, smallpox, pneumonia of one type or another, polio, for which bad cases had to be put in an iron lung, and scarlet fever. Sore throats developed into tonsillitis and then to scarlet fever. You could get sulphonamide compounds, but penicillin was not available. It was only just starting to be used in the forces. Tuberculosis was common and notices on buses stated 'Do not spit, penalty £5'. Smoking was only allowed on the upper deck.

Christmas fare consisted of a couple of chickens, usually from Uncle Snowie. He kept several at the bottom of his garden, mainly for the eggs. We did too, but after a fox had the lot we never bothered again.

A couple of rabbits were also part of the Christmas treat. These were hung in the kitchen with the chickens. The rabbits still had their fur on but were gutted, and the chickens were untouched until Christmas Eve. If you were lucky enough to get a ham, a whole leg, this was salted in a tin bath, the one used for bathing in front of the fire once a week.

I remember my uncle's chickens very well; not the hens particularly, but a very cocky cockerel. I still have scars on my legs fifty years later to remind me. I was playing in his garden by the back door just before Christmas when this cockerel ran at me with wings flapping and head down. I backed off towards the kitchen door and screamed, but not before he had pecked a bit out of my knee and dealt me a couple of deep scratches with his talons and spurs. My mother, hearing the screams, opened the back door and threw a cup of hot cocoa at the bird. It backed off sufficiently to allow her to grab me and pull me inside. My uncle decided to deal with the bird. 'Bugger keeps getting out and having a go' he said, 'Even attacking Fluffy'. Fluffy was their dog. He went to the tool shed, kicking at the bird on his way, and came out with three feet of two-by-four timber. We were watching from the kitchen and dining room windows. Snowie turned around. The bird went for my uncle, but he executed a smart cricket cover drive that knocked the cockerel several feet away. It did not move. My uncle approached cautiously, but as he got to within a foot of the cockerel it ruffled its feathers and took off into the air, aiming at my uncle's head. Another good swipe with the two by four caught the bird on the head. It fell to the ground obviously dazed, and my uncle quickly grabbed it and wrung its neck. We had the cockerel cooked for Christmas, but it was inedible. 'Bloody tough as old boots,' said my uncle. He gave it to Fluffy!

We still went to school regardless of the occasional air raid siren. The walk was about half a mile, but sometimes we had to make a decision whether to run back home or continue to school, whichever was nearest when the siren sounded. There was a brick shelter in the playground at our school, Westbury School, close to the road. During a raid the teachers would be outside the shelter waiting for stragglers and helping them across the road to the shelter. Because of rationing traffic was practically non-existent, not that there were many cars on the roads then anyway. Sometimes the siren went during classes and we would be led in an orderly fashion down into the school cellars. Here there were bunks with metal mesh bases to sit or lie on. We would sit on these and have our lessons until the all-clear siren. Usually we would be reciting our times tables, because I don't think the teachers could concentrate on our usual lessons.

Odd contraptions turned up in the streets from time to time. I saw a mobile gun parked at the end of our road, close to the junction of River Road. I did not hear it firing and it was gone the following morning.

Another piece of defence apparatus appeared quite close to our door. It looked like a small boiler on wheels with a long chimney. Apparently the boiler was lit from underneath and was intended to create a lot of smoke during an air raid, supposedly to obscure targets. It certainly made smoke. I do not know how successful it was, but when the wind changed it was choking. This contraption disappeared after a few days. (Years later I saw parts of it in the mud of the River Roding at the back of our houses.)

The river mud was a dark grey colour. One night during an air raid there was a huge explosion. 'Sounds like they are bombing the wharves at the back of us,' said my father. There were no other explosions, but this one seemed to lift the shelter off the ground. In the morning, out in the street, we gazed upon grey roofs and grey spattered streets. The explosion had been caused by a land mine dropped by parachute into the River Roding when the tide was out.

These land mines were big. My father told me that one had come down near my grandmother's in Dagenham and was caught up by the parachute hanging from the chimney stack of a house. The area was evacuated and a bomb disposal squad tried to defuse it, but tragically it exploded.

On occasional weekends we went by train to Shoeburyness, near Southend. Part of Shoeburyness was out of bounds because the army had taken it over. However we mostly travelled to Laindon with my uncles, aunts and cousins. Sometimes we stayed the whole weekend. My father and uncles had to go back on the Sunday however because of their work. We travelled there from Barking station by steam train, and I can remember posters on the station walls saying, 'Is your journey really necessary?'

If the carriage was full small children were put up in the luggage rack. This we enjoyed, although the string netting became uncomfortable after a while. On the journey we all carried bags containing food, drinks, sheets, blankets and a change of clothes. From the railway station at Laindon we had to walk a couple of miles through the country lanes; some parts of the lanes were concreted but most were just bridleways across fields.

When we were about a mile from the station my brother and I would usually say to Uncle Snowie, 'Are you strong today Uncle?' 'Yeah,' he would reply. 'Arm muscles like sparrers' kneecaps.' 'Well grab hold of these bags then' we would say and loop the bags over his arms and run. 'Cheeky little buggers!' was his usual retort.

Uncle Snowie and Uncle Fred owned about a quarter of an acre of land between them, and they each built huts on their parts of the plot, about twelve feet by six with a small shed for tools outside and another small shed as a toilet. The small tool shed had a slanted roof with a gutter and rainwater was collected in a water butt after it had passed through two boxes containing gravel and one with sand, as filters. The water was clear and potable. In Snowie's hut there were chairs that folded, a table and a couple of fold-up beds. The toilet was a bucket in the other small shed and contained Izal fluid. When the bucket was full a hole was dug in the corners of the plot and the contents buried.

Snowie's hut was 'clinker-built' with wooden planks and painted green. The base of the hut was concreted. The hut itself was supported at each corner and along the sides with bricks about six inches high leaving a gap underneath the hut.

The front door was a work of art. The top half of the door was a panel of leaded glass of many colours, home-made, I think, but the 'pièce de resistance' was the door handle. It was a large four to five-inch diameter knob of cut glass. Incongruous and ostentatious, but Snowie was proud of it.

It was very quiet and peaceful in the Laindon countryside. No wireless, no sirens, just birdsong. During the depression in the 1920s my uncles, being out of work with very little money, used to spend time in the huts with just a loaf or two of bread. Some of this bread was used as bait. It was sprinkled out in front of the huts and when the starlings or an occasional pigeon came to feed they were shot with an old Diana air rifle. There was very little meat on them, but it helped.

The plots were fenced with wooden stakes and plants. Our old clothes were kept in the hut in a box. My brother and I had little red 'wellie boots', which we wore all the time in Laindon. I remember the wellies well because in the 1960s I went back to Laindon on a nostalgic visit; the new town of Basildon was being built and most of the houses in and around Laindon were being demolished. On arrival at the plot I found the huts had just been knocked down and were burning on a large bonfire. Amongst the contents of the hut burning away I noticed my little red wellie boots, but I could not get to them because of the heat. Aaah!

I mentioned this to my Uncle Snowie and he was very upset, not because of my red wellies but because he was unaware that his land and his hut had been taken. It came to light that my Uncle Fred, who owned the other half of the land, had sold it to the authorities and it was assumed somewhere down the chain of command that it was the whole plot. I believe my uncle got some compensation, but very little and it took a lot of haggling. He would never have allowed his plot to go, but it was too late.

Late one afternoon in Laindon, my aunts and the children decided to go blackberry picking and search for mushrooms. Ethel called out to Snowie, who declined the trip, 'Look after the paraffin stove and don't fall asleep, the wick is high' she said.

Snowie was sitting in a deck chair in the hut. The paraffin stove was a tall chimney-like contraption with a 'mica' door for access to the wick and a flat-ridged top to take a saucepan or kettle. The wick was about two inches wide and made of canvas and had to be trimmed occasionally. It was regulated with a screw to lower or increase the flame.

We were out blackberrying for about two hours. When we got back we could see that the windows had turned black. Aunt Ethel opened the door, looked in and quickly stepped back, shaking with laughter. Snowie was still in the deckchair, fast asleep. Black strings of soot were floating in the air and hanging from the ceiling, the curtains and the shelves. They were also hanging from Snowie's eyebrows and chin and from his Roman nose. As he snored with his mouth wide open the strings of soot, long ones from his eyebrows and nose, would waft in and out of his mouth with every intake and exhalation.

He awoke to the sound of laughter and squeals from us. Ethel then called him a stupid old sod and got to work with my other aunt and my mother to clean the place up.

My cousin George, Snowie's son, was a lot older than my brother and me. He was in his teens and was in the Army Cadet Corps. One weekend he brought a friend with him to Laindon. His friend to us seemed very fastidious and was very much aware of the damp patches and grease inside the hut. He was careful to put paper down before he sat down on a bench or chair. He was not very talkative either.

It was raining hard and everyone was crowded into the hut. My brother, cousins and I were drawing pictures with pencil stubs in old office ledgers with red-lined pages. We were scattered on the floor and under the table, which took up more than half the hut. My mother and Aunt Ethel, with the help of Aunt Lucy, were cooking the meal on the paraffin stove and a primus stove. The hut was very steamy. My other uncle, Fred, and Aunt Nance were in the other hut on their plot of land with my cousin Michael having their meal.

The cooking done, the table was laid with a chequered oilcloth. The meal was served on the plates and placed on the table. I think there were about ten of us sitting around the table as well as we could manage with no elbowroom at all. Either side of the table, lengthwise, were two wooden benches that could be folded away. At each end of the table were two chairs and stools.

The noise on the tarpaulin roof was loud. We were all seated and were tucking into our stew with dumplings. Cousin George's friend, I do not remember his name, was picking at his food whilst everyone else was well into the stew with gusto. Suddenly there appeared a steady stream of water from the ceiling, landing at the end of the table and splashing those nearest. It got worse. Aunt Ethel swore. 'Can't you do something about it Snowie?' she said. 'All right, hang on, I'll fix it' said Snowie. He got up from the table, grabbed a piece of linoleum from the floor and another from the shelf behind him. Then he went out to the shed where he kept his tools, grabbed a hammer and stuffed some nails into his mouth, propped an old wooden ladder up the side of the hut and climbed onto the roof.

We could hear him clambering around and then a crashing and banging as he began hammering the lino to the roof. As he hammered the whitewash from the ceiling began to flake off and rain down on us. It fell everywhere, on our heads and onto our stew, most of it unfortunately on cousin George's friend. This caused great merriment. Snowie, when he came back in, was soaked, but he sat down without a word and proceeded to eat his stew, laughing and flicking off the whitewash with his knife.

We all got on with our meal unconcerned, except George's friend. He did not think the ghost-like diners covered in whitewash were funny at all. However the leak had stopped. George's friend did not finish his stew and he never made a second visit.

The banks of the River Roding, before it reaches the Barking bypass bridge at the back of the Bird's Eye custard factory, were lined with reeds on both sides. During the lull in air raids we were allowed to roam further afield. Our main pursuits were rat hunting with catapults or digging up bottles from the old bottle tip, throwing them in the river and then trying to sink them with good hits from our catapults. The bottles had been dumped there years ago and were well covered with earth and grass. They are probably still buried there today.

This whole area was known as 'the Dump'. 'Where are you off to?' 'Going over the Dump' was the usual reply. The source of ammunition for our catapults was pebbles from the bank of the river, where we made a small pebble beach by breaking down some of the bank. Our parents occasionally accompanied us, if the weather was fine. We sat on the little beach and even went for a swim if the tide was not going out.

The ebbing tide was very fast and dangerous. One time four boys, not from our area, made a raft out of a couple of old oil drums and wooden planks tied together with string and some rope. They tied it to a bollard on the concrete quayside close to our little beach, but the rope snapped and they were whisked away and the raft disintegrated. There was only one survivor, a ginger-haired boy, and he only survived because by chance a man saw him rushing past with the outgoing tide. He leant over the side of the quay, grabbed the boy by his hair as he went past and pulled him in. The bodies of the other three, I believe, were recovered somewhere near Tilbury or Gravesend.

On the Dump we dug square holes in the ground over about the same area as an air raid shelter, then covered them with pieces of timber, driftwood and old pieces of corrugated iron as a roof. Turfs were then laid on the roof, making a good camouflage. From only a short distance away the camp looked like a small hillock. To get inside we had to crawl along a tunnel, similarly covered in turf. Inside we built a small fireplace, dug into the walls and lined with rusty old sheets of tin. By bending this tin into a tube we fashioned a chimney. This was never efficient, and cooking potatoes on the fire, although great fun, was more of an eye-watering experience than a mouth-watering one.

In late autumn we would pick armfuls of large mushrooms, which we gave to the local general store on the corner opposite the fire station in exchange for sweets.

There were no bombers now, but the sirens still wailed to warn us of 'Doodlebugs', the V1 rockets. The deep throaty pulsating noise of the V1 was very distinctive. It was powered by a pulse-jet engine on top and to the rear of the fuselage housed the explosive. I can still quite accurately imitate the sound of the V1 now!

The Doodlebugs were indiscriminate and very destructive and London was a big target. From our little pebble beach we could watch them on their way up the river towards the city. The engine gave a loud guttural, staccato note, and when the engine cut out and the V1 started to dive we could see where it was going to drop. That was when you became anxious.

Whenever the family visited the Dump my Aunt Lucy would lie face down on the ground when the engine cut out, regardless of where the Doodlebug was. This however did not start until after D-Day, June 1944.

Our housing area was close to the river and the small warehouses and docks along the River Road. From my back garden mobile and fixed cranes could be seen loading and unloading small ships and barges, usually with timber. In ancient times pirates and smugglers used the River Roding, and the Saxon abbey was destroyed by Danes in the ninth century travelling up the river to the Barking quay area. In the 18th Century Captain James Cook, the explorer and navigator, was married in Barking to a local girl.

Incidentally Grandfather Styles was a lighterman on the Thames and used to work on the barges up and down the river. Not only was he more often than not drunk, I was told he could not swim a stroke. Small tugs used to pull dozens of fully laden barges two or three abreast along the river, and against the tide they hardly seemed to move. The tugs manoeuvring them against the tide were likened to a duck with her ducklings.

To get to the Dump we usually went to my grandmother's house, where my uncle Bob and aunt Elsie lived with my cousin Ronnie. We went through the fence at the back, climbed up a bank and then to the little beach. The houses were I think about twenty feet lower than the river. Alternatively we could go through my Uncle Snowie's garden in Westminster Gardens, which was further along the river towards the Barking bypass, and we 'scrumped' his apples on the way.

My father at this time worked at the gasworks in Beckton and travelled there on his bicycle. Sometimes he was away for a couple of days. He was in the Home Guard, and occasionally he came home in uniform with a Lee Enfield .303 rifle. He showed me the working parts of the rifle and how to use it, but never with any ammunition about. He only had one round in the five-round clip and the rifle was too heavy for my brother and me to lift with any ease. When he came home in his uniform he occasionally brought home wooden toys, aeroplanes, boats and tanks. These were carved, I was told, by German prisoners of war. He also gave me a rusty German Luger pistol, the firing pin of which he had removed. Where the POWs were imprisoned I never found out.

Most toys for boys during the war were guns, mostly 'Tommy guns'. They could make a noise, because they had a ratchet similar to the rattles used at football matches. When you turned the handle at the side of the gun it went rat-tat-tat like a machine gun. Wooden toys, whether tanks or cricket stumps, bails and bats, were often made by our parents.

About a week or so after D-Day in June 1944, the air raid sirens started up again. No bombers this time but as previously mentioned the Doodlebug era had begun. The Barking Park ack-ack had started and the Creekmouth guns too, so shrapnel collectors were in business again.

The ack-ack guns were successful, with the help of radar, along the south coast and the Creekmouth. Balloons were only helping to bring them down on a target anyway, so my father said. Most successful were the Hurricanes and Spitfires and later the Gloster Meteor jets and the Hawker Tempests, which were able to shoot them down because of their greater speed. Apart from shooting them down they could move them off course into an unpopulated area by tipping them with their wing tips. It was a great thrill to see these aircraft, especially the Gloster Meteor jets, the first jets we had ever seen. If we heard the engine cut out and we were close, we would dive into our shelter. The time lapse was about ten seconds before the explosion. This was all right if we were out in the open by the River Roding where we could watch their progress from the Creekmouth. From the streets, when the 'music' stopped, we could not always see them, so we dashed to the dugout.

One weekend, playing outside my Grandmother Styles' house with friends and cousins, the siren went. With the siren still wailing everyone started getting indoors and out the back to the shelter. We were calling and looking down the street for any stragglers. 'Where's Kay?' said my mother. 'Isn't she in the house?' I said. 'No' said my aunt, 'She's out on the little bike.'

I dashed through the front gateway, jumped on my small two-wheeler and pedalled like mad down the street and round the corner. As I rounded the corner there was Kay running towards me, the little three-wheeler behind her in the kerb. As we reached each other I swung the bike around, grabbed her and lifted her onto the crossbar. I then pedalled furiously towards my mother and aunt, who were standing by the gate waving anxiously for us to hurry. I stopped my bike with a squeal from the old brakes. My aunt grabbed Kay, who was about four years old, and started to run through the house to the shelter. Throwing the bike in the kerb, I was immediately behind them with my mother close after me. The engine noise stopped and before my mother and I could reach the shelter the ground heaved and there was a great explosion. It had landed about a quarter of a mile away near the town quay.

In early June 1944, whilst crossing the Barking bypass opposite the fire station, I saw convoys of Bren gun carriers and army vehicles including tanks travelling along the road, and flying overhead were Dakotas towing white-striped marked gliders. At the time I was not aware how significant this was. They were of course off to take part in the top-secret D-Day landings of June 6th.

Westbury School was about half a mile away from home. To get there we passed the Volunteer pub, crossed over the Barking bypass, Alfred's Way and down Movers Lane with Greatfields Park on the left. At the end of the park there was a public toilet and across the road an off licence. A further few hundred yards to Ripple Road, we crossed the road to the school. There was very little traffic. Not many people owned cars and those who did could not get the petrol, as previously mentioned. That was rationed too. There was the occasional car with a large gasbag on the roof as a fuel source. So apart from air raids we could play in the streets with safety.

My friend and neighbour Fred, my brother and I were on our way to school and had reached the mid-point of our journey, half way along Movers Lane, close to the toilets and the 'offie' when the siren went. What should we do? Fred decided immediately to run back home and being a fast runner, off he went. My brother and I took off towards the school. We had only gone a few yards when we heard the growl of a Doodlebug. As we ran we heard it getting louder and louder. Turning around and looking over our shoulders, we saw it, coming straight over our houses where Fred was running. As we started to cross Ripple Road to get to the school we could see Mr Coe, one of our teachers, waving at us to hurry. We were running as fast as we could. We did not need much encouragement! We raced across the road and through the school gates into the playground, where there was a brick shelter close to the railings. (For some reason the iron railings were not removed for the war effort as most were.) As we got to the shelter the V1's engine stopped and seconds later we felt and heard the explosion. It was very close. After the siren sounded the all-clear, Fred turned up at school and said it was a direct hit on the public toilets. (In the sixties he played cricket for England.) On the way home from school we had to go through the park. That part of Movers Lane was closed off and there were many ARP and policemen at the scene. The shops across the road from the park had broken windows and frames, the glass still hanging from the crisscrossed sticky tape used for this very eventuality. There were a few roof tiles scattered around. But most noticeable was the off-licence. It was only half there, but that was more than could be said for the toilets – they had vanished. Along the street were great chunks of porcelain that would never have 'Percy' pointing at them again. Parts of the Doodlebug could be seen around. The pulse-jet engine seemed intact, as was one of the short wings. The following morning all had disappeared except for the large hole in the ground.

In September 1944 we experienced our first V2 rocket (the V stands for 'Vergeltungswaffen' or reprisal weapon). Where the Doodlebug was 26 feet long with a wingspan of 18 feet, the V2 was 46 feet long and 6 feet in diameter with no wings, just tail fins. This was the predecessor to the space rockets used today. They had a trajectory which took them up to 100,000 feet and travelled at 3600 miles per hour. The V2 did not have a nickname like the V1, possibly because it was never seen – you only heard it coming, as it were, after it had hit its target and exploded, as it was travelling faster than sound. It took only minutes from launch to target. It weighed 12 tonnes and was fuelled by alcohol and liquid oxygen.

One Sunday morning, instead of going to Sunday school at the Congregational church known to me as St. Paul's near the Barking Broadway, Blakes Corner, I was told to go and get some vegetables. My mother was entertaining relations that afternoon. The church was made of flintstone and stood near the library opposite Pesci Brothers' fish and chip shop. They had a plate glass etching of a haddock or cod across the frontage. I was sent to Oakes, the greengrocers, to get lettuce and cucumbers to go with our pilchards, winkles and cockles for tea. Oakes was usually open on Sunday mornings. The shop was a couple of minutes away from the church. I cycled to the shop via Gascoigne Road, but I had only just reached the shop when there was a huge blast that knocked me off my bike. I was dazed but otherwise unhurt. I found myself in the doorway of an adjoining shop with boiled sweets all around me. My bike however was somewhat twisted. Pesci Brothers' window was intact – the shop is still there as I write.

I was helped to my feet, still a little dazed and a little deaf. The V2 had hit the church, killing four children I knew and some adults. I looked up the street towards what was left of the church. Half was still standing and prominent in my mind is the memory of a dustbin on what was left of the roof.

I was checked over by a shopkeeper and an ARP man. I picked up my bent bike and carried it towards home minus vegetables. I had just started when I saw my father running towards me. He grabbed hold of me and my bike and strode off down the road. I do not remember him saying much except 'You all right Brian?'

My father left his job at the gasworks to work on a dredger on the Thames for the Port of London Authority. He once took my brother and me, when he was on weekend caretaker duty, to stay the weekend on board. The ship was a bucket dredger 'Hopper' 14. It was very exciting for my brother and me, especially so as my father had to row us from the quayside to the dredger moored to a couple of buoys with large chains in the middle of the river. The tide was going out and the speed of the current made it necessary for my father to start rowing and sculling very hard a few hundred yards downriver. The timing had to be pretty good, otherwise we might have finished up near Gravesend.

The dredger had three cranes, two forward and one aft in front of the bridge. There was also a walkway between the cranes and over the large hold amidships. When the hold was full the load would be dumped further upriver near the Thames estuary, by opening the keel doors like the bomb bay doors on a Wellington or Lancaster bomber.

My brother and I slept in bunks and during the day played in the wheelhouse pretending to steer the ship. We investigated the ship from stem to stern. We played hide and seek using every part of the ship including chain lockers and engine room. I can recall the smell of mud and rusty iron now. We were happy and very privileged.

Approximately once a week a man wheeled a barrow through

the streets selling fish, winkles, shrimps, cockles and whelks. I loved whelks as a kid and I still do.

There was also a horse and cart loaded with fruit and veg, mainly plums and apples when in season, otherwise just vegetables. I had never seen a banana and rarely an orange. Laindon trips were helpful, we used to bring back apples and blackberries and some raspberries grown on the plot.

Just before the end of the war the greengrocer was trading along Craven Gardens. For some unknown reason the horse managed to break loose from its harness and bolted down the street with the greengrocer shouting and chasing after it. It ran past me and my friends playing in the street and turned right into Westminster Gardens towards the Barking bypass opposite the fire station, where there were usually buses and lorries going back and forth. A couple of men gave chase on hearing the commotion. One man further along Westminster Gardens, wearing only pyjamas and socks, shot out from his front garden. He must have seen the horse from his window. I don't think he was gardening in his pyjamas and socks. He ran fast and caught up with the horse at the corner before it reached the bypass. He grabbed the trailing reins and blinkers and stopped it. The old greengrocer, puffing and sweating, reached them eventually, shook the man by the hand and without a word walked the horse back to the cart, hitched it up and continued trading.

On one trip to Laindon the train stopped before we got there for about half an hour because of an air raid. The train was crowded with passengers going to Thorpe Bay, Canvey Island, Southend or Shoeburyness. These destinations were popular because of the beaches. Other beaches along the south coast were out of bounds and protected with barbed wire and concrete tank traps in case of an invasion.

The crowded train was very quiet. My mother was talking to my Aunt Lucy. 'Is there any soap in the hut?' said my aunt. 'I've brought some with me,' said my mother, and showed her. 'Oh, you've brought your toothbrushes as well!' said my aunt. My little cousin Kay saw them. 'I had one of those once' she said, 'but the feathers fell out.' This started giggles and laughter from everyone in the packed carriage. The train started off again when it got a green signal, to the relief of everyone.

I remember the soap very well. At the end of the day in Laindon, when it was time to go back to Barking, we lined up in front of a tin bowl of hot water to be cleaned with a flannel and soap. For some reason the soap always got impregnated with grit and sand. The rough towel to dry us was not much better. No mercy was given. It was like being smoothed down with sandpaper. I have to say we all looked rosy and polished, albeit a little sore after the ordeal.

My uncle Fred was a master welder and worked for Standard Telephones. He was sent to Somerset and lived in Ilminster with the firm, to escape the bombings I imagine. He also occasionally helped out on the farms. He had a dog but a farm worker, who said it was worrying the sheep, shot it. Fred denied this and one dark night, he caught the farm worker down an alley and gave him more than a bloody nose. He got himself another dog, a mongrel but with a high percentage of whippet in its makeup.

We were spending a week's holiday with Uncle Fred. One day it was decided we would take a bus ride to some recreational fields with a lake and have a picnic. It was a few miles away and would take over half an hour. We boarded the bus along with boxes of food and bottles of Tizer and cream soda. The bus started off and after about a mile, someone in the back seat said 'There's a dog chasing after us'. We all looked through the back window and in the distance we could see Fred's dog going flat out after us. The bus however increased the distance between the dog and us. Each time we rounded a corner, and there were many of them, we lost sight of the dog, but when we came to a straight section of road the dog was seen coming round the corner at speed, still going flat out but not gaining on us. The passengers cheered every time it came into sight. This went on for a couple of miles, then my Aunt Nance intervened. She thought the dog had probably had enough and asked the driver very firmly to stop the bus and take the dog on board. This he did. When the dog reached us my aunt pulled it on board and put it between the seats in the gangway. We had no water to give it. The dog was panting and gasping, making quite a noise and the lolling tongue dribbling a large pool on the floor.

Its thirst was soon remedied when we reached our destination shortly afterwards. The dog jumped out of the bus and raced straight to the lake.

We had our picnic and did some paddling along the water's edge. We were lazing about on the grass when two soldiers came over to us and started chatting. Their accents were strange and their uniforms smart and of a smooth material unlike my father's battledress uniform of rough khaki.

They were American and they were relaxing before their departure to France on D-Day. They offered cigarettes to my aunt and mother. My Aunt Nance took one but my mother did not smoke. I was shown a dollar bill, which the soldier tore in half and gave one half to my brother and the other to me. This was indeed a prize to take back to Barking. I sometimes wonder if either of them survived.

The only time during the week in Somerset when we were reminded of the war was when occasionally one could see in the sky vapour trails crisscrossing where our planes were dog fighting. My uncle usually called us indoors in case of falling debris from the aircraft.

One Sunday at our house, with relations sitting round the dining room table after evening dinner playing cards, I remember another family being present. There was a tall man about six foot; his wife was very short and they had a daughter a little older than myself. I think my mother used to go swimming with this man. I remember going a couple of times to the indoor pool near the Barking town hall. The open-air pool in Barking Park was not available as the ack-ack was stationed there.

We began to see this family quite often. We got on well but I did not like the man very much, for reasons I could not at the time explain.

One afternoon my mother got my brother and me dressed up to go to the city. 'We're going to the Lyons Corner House' she said. What a treat, a trip and meal in the West End of London and a chance to see the bomb damage!

We walked to the bus stop opposite the fire station. My mother said 'Uncle George' [the tall man] is going to meet us there'. I said 'I'm not going then' and started to run home. My mother caught up with me and pleaded. She said 'He loves us very much and would like us to live together'. I was furious and very upset. My brother seemed unconcerned and did not react at all. However we went to Lyons Corner House and met him there. We ordered fish and chips and I had rock eel, my favourite.

Whilst waiting for the meal to arrive my brother and I began to get a bit fidgety and were playing with our knives and forks. 'Stop playing with the cutlery and sit up straight' said Uncle George firmly. I stared at him and said 'You're not my father'. My mother told me to be quiet. I obeyed and ate my fish and chips in silence, but I did not enjoy it one little bit. On the way home very little was said.

Some time later there was a terrible atmosphere at home and with my relations. My mother had fallen in love with 'Uncle' George but she would not leave my brother and me to be with him. She decided to stay with my father and us and make a go of it as a family. This situation came to a tragic end shortly after the war ended. This 'uncle' must have been very much in love with my mother and vice versa. When he heard the news that it was all over between him and my mother, he committed suicide by putting his head in a gas oven. There was sadness in the family for a long time and what his wife and daughter must have felt was difficult for me to understand. Today I can better understand my mother and what she sacrificed and the devotion she had for my brother and me. This of course was a very traumatic time for my father also. He loved my mother regardless.

We followed the D-Day advances with great interest. I had a map on the wall above my bed on which I plotted the progress of our advance by sticking pins in it. I gathered information from newspapers and news from the wireless. The wireless was well used, particularly when ITMA (It's That Man Again) was on. The kids in the street picked up all the catch phrases used by Tommy Handley and his gang. 'Can I do yer now sir?', from Mrs Mop. 'I don't mind if I do sir', Colonel Chinstrap and many others. Music was mainly songs from Vera Lynn, Joe Loss, Victor Sylvester and Petula Clark. Not one of the ITMA programmes was missed.

Songs sung by Vera Lynn were 'There'll be bluebirds over the white cliffs of Dover', 'Wish me luck as you wave me goodbye' and 'It's a long way to Tipperary'. We loved, as kids, to sing this song to the tune of Colonel Bogey:

Hitler has only got one ball
Goring has one but very small
Himmler has something similar
But poor old Goebbels has no balls at all.

When the war ended VE Day was celebrated with street parties everywhere and all the children were dressed up by their parents in fancy dress. I do not know who or what I was supposed to be, but I had a red, white and blue jacket and a black top hat with ribbons. I do remember the hat was too big and kept falling over my eyes. Everyone had a great time with loads of food supplied by the parents and lots of orange juice and Tizer. The grown-ups were drinking plenty of beer and tots of rum and whisky.

Trestle tables were assembled down the middle of the street and covered with cloth from one end to the other with benches to sit on. Lamp posts were decorated, as were most of the houses. The tables were laden with sandwiches, jellies and cakes. There was music from gramophones and some of the parents were dancing. After the food had been eaten the tables were cleared away and two huge bonfires were made up at both ends of the street and set alight. These bonfires were kept going all night and the kids were, to our delight, allowed to stay out late. The parents were enjoying themselves drinking and dancing and we were busy roasting potatoes on sticks in the bonfires. This was hot work because the bonfires were huge. Today the area where the bonfires were can still be seen. There is a large circular red patch on the concrete road scorched by the heat of the bonfire, but of course the roads might be now covered in Tarmac.

The war for the Shrapnel kids was not quite over, as Japan was still fighting. We played in the streets as usual, but now doors were closed. 'Stop that bloody row! Why don't you go and play down your own end of the street?' This was now becoming the norm.

My father, still working on the dredger, occasionally brought home various interesting bits and pieces that were picked up by the crane grabs from the mud. Sometimes it was old cartridge belts and once an old flintlock rifle. Most of the wooden parts were missing or rotted away and the metal well-rusted. He also brought home a handful of bullets minus the cartridge casing.

One day my brother and I with a friend, Don, were playing with lead soldiers in front of the fire in the living room. We had tanks, guns and lorries. This back living room faced the garden and lean-to. My friend was right in front of the fire with a toy soldier. The soldier was kneeling on one knee with a shell ready to load into a Howitzer. My brother was on the settee in front of the window. For some unknown reason, to this day I do not know what possessed me, I tossed two of the bullets my father had brought home on the fire. Nothing happened and we forgot all about them. Then after about fifteen minutes, with my friend still in front of the fire with the kneeling lead soldier, one of the bullets exploded with a flash and a large bang that deafened us. The fire was blown out of the fireplace. My brother started screaming. The settee and the curtains were alight. My friend was miraculously untouched but the lead soldier he was playing with had lost its head.

I was standing against the wall by the door. My mother had heard the bang and the screams from my brother and came rushing in, slamming the door open and flattening me against the wall. My nose started to bleed and I felt dazed, seeing little bright dots swimming around. She was shouting but we could not at first hear her properly. The explosion had deafened us. I managed to convey to her that there was another bullet on the fire. The lodger from upstairs came down and helped put out the burning furniture. My mother then threw all of us, almost literally, out of the room. She grabbed a dustbin lid and filled a bowl with water and with a poker began to poke around what was left of the fire in the grate. She soon found the other bullet, which was red hot and a little distorted. She poured water on it and left the room. She did not scold us. She obviously thought we had learnt our lesson. However my father did not get away without a good ear-bashing when he came home. Apparently the bullets were from an aircraft and one was a tracer. Perhaps the other one was too, but fortunately we did not find out.

A week or so later my father bought us some boxing gloves and started teaching my brother and me how to box. It did not last long, however. My father was sparring with me in the living room. My mother was sitting in an armchair knitting. He stepped back on my mother's toe at the very moment that my right fist was on its way. As he turned round concerned about my mother's toe, I caught him square on the jaw. He was knocked out cold.

After the war, we were allowed fireworks for the first time. This was the first Guy Fawkes night we ever had as children and it was very exciting. We bought bangers and rockets mainly, some large, but mostly small. Fireworks started to be let off at least a couple of days before November 5th. One of the boys stood a rocket up in a milk bottle and then tied a cannon, a large banger, onto the stick of the rocket just below the rocket head. He lit the rocket first and when it began to fizz he lit the blue touch paper on the banger. The rocket took off, but with the weight of the banger it only went rooftop high and careered over the roof of my Aunt Rose's house into her back garden. We all stood wide-eyed, waiting for the bang. After less than a minute it went off, very loud. Almost immediately my Aunt came running out shouting, 'You've killed one of my chickens!' Apparently a curious hen had taken a peck at the banger just as it went off. Ah well! Fewer eggs, but there was roast chicken for my cousins' Sunday dinner.

Shortly after the war we all went on holiday to Hastings, our first big holiday, with Snowie, Ethel, Daisy, Sylvie and Iris. Cousin George was not present. It was a very hot week and I remember it well because Sylvie stayed out in the sun too long and I remember on the bus that she could not move and was suffering from sunstroke. She kept swearing and dribbling and we had to cover her in calamine lotion.

Our air raid shelter was dismantled soon after VE and VJ day. The only part that was left was the square concrete hole. My father half filled it with rubble and cemented over the top. This was then filled with water to turn it into a pond. In the bottom, before the cement had set, a jar with the bottom knocked out was pushed through the concrete to the lip of the jar. By taking off the screw cap we could let the water drain away if it became necessary.

This was the start of my fascination with pond life and biology in general. I bought a brass microscope for £2 10s (£2.50). It was just a straight brass one with telescopic drawtube and one nosepiece lens apart from the eyepiece lens. Although old and probably worth a bit today, it was not very easy to use, so after a while I saved up £4 10s and purchased a better one. This had a wooden case and was also made of brass. It had rack and pinion fine and coarse focusing with movable stage controls, plus a triple lens nosepiece. I studied the flora and fauna of ponds and became quite knowledgeable.

Chapter 2

Schooldays

The year after the war ended, sports were resumed at school, cricket and football. At Westbury School in one of the cupboards, green football shirts and socks were found. They had a musty smell and the socks were very holed. They were washed and cleaned and darned by our parents. Football boots with the leather studs to be nailed on were first on the list for Christmas.

We won almost every match in the 1946-47 period, and we played in the final against Dorothy Barley school on the Barking Football Club ground in front of a crowd of parents. We lost one–nil. We received bronze medals from the mayor and had our photos taken.

We won every match however at cricket and won the shield. I was one of the top scorers, but Fred Rumsey was by far our best bowler. Later he turned professional and played county cricket and was picked for England in a test match against the Kiwis in the 1960s.

During the weekends we still played in the streets but travelled further afield, down the Creekmouth or catching a tram to Abbey

Wood or Pitsea, where we climbed chalk cliffs. The trams were very noisy but fun. The driver sat at the front with his brass steering handle. The arms on the roof connected to the overhead electric cable, similar to trolleybuses, and they often came adrift. When the tram reached the terminus it did not turn around. The driver went to the back end, which was the same as the front, reversed the arms, pulled the backs of the seats over so they faced the other way (they were wooden slatted seats), and we were off again.

Some of the double-decker buses, the 106, 175 and 23c, still had an open-backed stairway with a brass rail. We occasionally disembarked by jumping out the back half way down the staircase.

At the Creekmouth we climbed pylons and swung between the upright supports with a rope that we had tied to a crossbar, climbing up by means of the metal pegs that the men used to get to the metal ladders further up and then to the platforms and the high-tension electric cables. One lad, not one of our friends, climbed one of the electric pylons and was dared to put two cups tied together by the handles over the wire. He touched them and was killed. Our games then were very dangerous, and today they would not be allowed.

During those days we seemed to have many fogs. These fogs were very thick indeed. They were known as pea-soupers, not just because they were thick but because of the colour, faintly yellow. You had to cover your face with a handkerchief, which quickly became black when breathed in. Our next-door neighbour had a daughter, Marjorie, who one very foggy evening crossed the Barking bypass from the fire station side to the Birds Custard Factory side. Because of the fog she became disorientated and could not see her hand stretched out in front of her. She could not find the other side of the road and must have walked down the side of the custard factory towards the river. She spent about an hour before she found the corner shop at the junction of Westminster Gardens and the bypass a few yards from where she started. She must have been going around in circles. She was very distressed when she eventually got home.

Our next-door neighbour just after the war bought a television and would ask us round when there was a play to watch. The television had a small screen but it had a large piece of Perspex in front as a magnifier. She was very houseproud and I was always very nervous; when I was offered a cup of tea I drank it as quickly as possible so that I did not have to hold it too long and risk spilling it. She bought a hall and stair carpet and had it laid, but so as not to wear it out too quickly the old carpet was laid on top, pile side down. This was beyond my comprehension. It looked horrible.

The winter of 1946-7 was cold and lasted for months with thick snow. It snowed for weeks and we used to build igloos in the streets. The main pursuit was the slide. This was kept going along the road and was about forty feet long. No one was allowed to use it with studded boots and parents would help by pouring water on it at night to keep it nice and smooth. They would also join in.

At the bridge on the Barking bypass that crossed the River Roding we used to use the steep banks as a toboggan run. Our toboggans were the 'J' shaped corrugated iron sides of the Anderson shelters. This was rather dangerous because with five or six boys and girls on board there were some that fell by the wayside and could get run over by other toboggans. The hardest part was dragging the heavy corrugated sheets back up to the top.

I passed my eleven-plus exam and took a course with engineering bias at the South West Essex Technical College in Walthamstow, starting at the annexe part of the college in Winns Avenue. Apart from my interest in biology and microscopy, my other hobby was painting, and I was also fascinated with ships and had pictures cut from the *Eagle* comic on my bedroom walls.

I saw very little of the shrapnel kids from then on, as we all went our separate ways career wise. I even lost touch with my school sweetheart June, although the pavements still showed the chalk marks JW-L-BE and vice-versa as I walked to Barking station to catch the steam train to Blackhorse Road station and then a bus to college.

After the war, before starting college, we still occasionally went over the Dump with catapults. We took sides and fired stones at each other but when someone got hit we realised how dangerous it was. I remember well the shock of a stone parting my hair. A direct hit might have killed us. We also visited the Creekmouth, now that the ack-ack guns had gone, leaving the brick gun emplacements for us to hide in and fire at each other with our catapults, which used 3/16th square rubber as used for model aircraft while the pouch was made from sections of an old cricket ball. This was scraped to make it pliable and holes burnt in the corners for the rubber bands and one in the centre to allow air to pass. They were extremely powerful. My cousin Michael once caught a ricochet through a brick window of the emplacements and had a bloody nose from pieces of brick. We decided enough was enough.

The 'dugouts' we built over the Dump were used for other reasons apart from cooking 'spuds' on the smoky fire, as we were growing up. Girls used to come to the camp. Sexual encounters, ie 'You show me yours and I'll show you mine', progressed to feeling the girls' firm breasts and the girls playing with the boys until they climaxed. For some, ejaculation had not begun. These first experiences were unforgettable and will remain in my memory, but the girl's names I have forgotten.

About this time my mother brought home a scruffy Pekinese dog, covered in fleas, which we called Mick. We had to give him a good clean. He had been with a family that had many other dogs and the woman wanted to get rid of him. We got on very well together and you could tell he had been with other dogs because he would not touch his food without a fight first. So I used to poke a broom at him and he would grab hold of the bristles and shake it like mad, growling and snorting through his snub nose. This lasted a couple of minutes and then he would calmly get on with his food.

Mick would wait at the gate for me to come home and run towards me when he spotted me. I became very attached to him, but a few years later he became somewhat arthritic and could not even get up a kerb.

Going to the technical college was very different from travelling to Westbury School. I had to walk to Barking station, then take a steam train to Blackhorse Road and a bus to Walthamstow town hall. This was quite a journey for a twelve-year-old. There were others though, I was not alone. They came from Dagenham and Barking, both boys and girls.

There were fifth formers who used to torment us on the journey home. They would tie us up with our neckties, put us on the luggage racks and then push us off so that we bounced on the seat below. We used to fight and some fights got pretty heated. However we gained some respect, even though we were smaller. Sometimes train windows got smashed. When this happened there was a mass exodus of college boys and girls jumping off the train before it came to a halt in the station.

The fifth formers also removed our shoes and tied them all together by the laces. When the train stopped at Barking Station, platform one, they waited for an underground train going to Upminster on platform two and threw the shoes on to it. We had to dash on quickly before the doors closed. We then spent ages untying the knots, to the amusement of the other passengers. We usually managed to get them untied before Hornchurch Station and then of course we had to catch a train back to Barking. Our parents never queried why we were sometimes late home. I was not very amused, because I always wanted to get my homework done and out of the way so as to pursue my hobbies. When we became fourth formers and the aforementioned fifth formers had left, life became a little more civilised.

We used to get into a carriage at Blackhorse Road to go home with the college girls to Barking and Dagenham. There was a lot of 'snogging', fondling of breasts etc. We of course had the blinds pulled down and at every station we opened them so that all looked normal. Passengers who wanted to get in found it difficult because we used to put our feet against the handles, making them difficult to turn. We resumed our 'play' when the train was again in motion.

One day on the way home I was having a good time with Eva, who wanted to be my girlfriend. We were kissing and fondling by the window with the blinds down as we were coming into Barking Station. I accidentally nudged the blind from its securing notch and it shot up. An electric underground train arriving on a parallel course heading for platform two passed only a couple of feet away, and all the passengers were grinning and gesticulating at Eva and me, who were red with embarrassment and dishevelled. Being caught with my hand down a girl's blouse and kissing in front of a trainload of people is difficult to forget.

Academically however I did quite well. With my engineering bias I did metalwork on lathes and also woodwork. Engineering drawing, algebra and geometry were our main subjects. I became form captain, captain of Newton House and games captain. I was also a prefect for a short time, but that was taken away because I refused to wear my school cap.

I was only caned once, and that was at the beginning of my time at college. It was because, after I had kicked a ball and smashed a window and was told to stop playing, I continued to play and smashed another window. Six of the best on your backside is not too bad. I played a lot of soccer, but I was very keen on rugby union football and played a bit in the park with friends from Park Modern School, who played 'rugger'.

I have fond memories of my school days, especially a geography lesson when the teacher asked the class to name exports from Denmark, starting with the back of the class going left to right. The first boy said 'timber, sir'; the second boy said 'cheese, sir'; the next boy said milk, the fourth butter and the fifth boy said bacon. The next boy was Tony and he was before me. Without hesitation, although to me the number of exports must have been exhausted, he said, 'fried bread sir'. I pictured in my mind a ship on its way with a hold and decks full of fried bread, and laughed uncontrollably. I laughed so much I was sent out of the classroom. I was still laughing in the corridor and was dragged off to the deputy head. He told me off and I stopped laughing. He sent me back to the classroom, where there were three other boys outside laughing. It started me off again, but fortunately the class ended.

Woodwork also holds fond memories. Our teacher in the woodwork class was Dutch, Mr Van der Something. One of the pupils, another Brian, did not like woodwork. He spent every lesson during the two years picking up wood shavings and sawdust and pressing them together in a vice so that they stuck together, like today's wood chipboards. He then broke them up with a hammer – pointless! This annoyed the teacher, who shouted at him 'If you have not finished making your serviette rings and stand by the end of the term you will be sent to the headmaster, understand?' 'Yes' mumbled Brian. The teacher was a little deaf and shouted 'Vat did you zay?' 'Yes I understand,' said Brian. He had just three weeks at three hours per week to complete the task of making six serviette rings and the pole stand that the rings dropped over. It was wintertime and a large pot-bellied stove heated the workshop that burnt coke fed by a hole in the top. The hole was covered by a metal plate lifted by a metal rod so as not to burn oneself. With one lesson to go, Brian managed to finish.

Mr Van der Something was poking the coke stove with a poker in one hand getting it really hot and holding the metal plate with the toggle bar in the other. Brian, holding his nine-inch pole carrying six serviette rings, walked up to the teacher to show him his work. 'I've finished sir.' he said. 'Vat?' said the teacher, not knowing that Brian was right behind him. He turned as Brian thrust his finished work in front of him at arm's length. The wooden serviette rings slid off the pole straight into the hole of the pot-bellied stove and fell into the blazing coke furnace. It took only minutes for them to be completely consumed.

The looks of horror on both Brian's and Mr Van der Something's face were too much for us. We could not stifle our laughter. The teacher grabbed the pole stand from Brian in fury, threw it onto the fire after the serviette rings, dismissed the class and without another word marched out of the woodwork shop. We were still holding onto the vices, convulsed, otherwise I think we would have collapsed.

We were not that keen on the geography lessons apart from the Danish export lesson. The college being large, we had to move to different classrooms for each lesson, so on our lesson chart the number of the classroom for each lesson had to be given. The geography lesson was often accompanied by slide projections of the geography master's holidays, which was a bore.

One day the class arrived early for the lesson and the teacher had as yet not turned up. We were on the second floor and we decided to pull down the blackout blinds and hide behind them, standing on the window shelves. We heard the teacher come in, put down his projection equipment and mutter to himself. After two to three minutes we heard footsteps and the closing of the door gave us leave to reappear. He did not return, and we played football in the quadrangle.

The boys and girls from Dagenham and Barking who travelled on the steam train to Walthamstow were labelled as the hooligan element at the college by some of the teachers. They were right in some respects, although some boys who were not from Barking or Dagenham were caught stealing from a shop and had a public caning, that is they were caned on their backsides on the stage in the main assembly hall in front of the whole school.

One boy riding his bike crashed into another boy in the college quadrangle and knocked him unconscious. Don, another Brian and I, all steam train commuters, quickly covered him with our maroon blazers, turned him on his side and put a rolled-up coat under his head, then sent someone off to get the matron. We were to be commended for our swift and thoughtful action in front of the whole school at morning assembly. Unfortunately, unknown to the headmaster, we were the same boys who were to be reprimanded for the reported hooliganism on the train. This caused some embarrassment for the headmaster but smiles from the teachers and snorts from the pupils. There were big grins from us as we stood up to be acclaimed and then reprimanded.

Instead of holidays to Hastings or Shoeburyness, we had a holiday on a river cruiser for a week. This was just before I left school. We hired a ten-berth boat to accommodate my father, mother, Uncle Fred, Aunt Nance, my brother Peter, cousins Michael, Gary and John and my school friend Brian. This was a trip from Crookham up the river through locks towards Oxford, and the boat was called the *Sirius Star*.

Uncle Fred and my friend Brian and I were keen on the fishing we hoped to have. The others were just excited to be on the boat and having a different sort of holiday. My father was the skipper and was given instructions on the workings of the cruiser before we were allowed on board. Lessons over, we clambered aboard in our Sunday best clothes. We got under way, heading for the first lock on the other side of the river. But as we approached the lock gates they started to close, and there was no way we could get there in time. My father, not as yet au fait with the boat's stopping distance and the allowance of way, steered towards the opposite bank to tie up to a huge mooring pile. We headed straight for one and found ourselves on a collision course, hardly slowing down even in reverse. Fred jumped to the bow and lying prone he stuck his feet out to soften the inevitable contact. The force of the contact pushed him back against the cockpit. We hit the pile nonetheless, and it creaked slowly backwards and then straightened, pushing us back again. However with engine stopped and Fred tying up on the pile, we were stationary. The fishermen on the banks were not too pleased, because we had sailed over their lines.

After less than half an hour the lock gates began to open again. I think this lock was the first and biggest on the Thames. We were going up a level. We slowly entered the lock and tied up. The gates closed and water began to rush in. There were people along the sides and on the lock gates watching the boats etc. When the lock was almost full of water the gatekeeper began to push on the bars and the gates slowly opened with a rush and a swirling of water. We let go fore and aft and pushing the boat from the side of the lock with boat hooks, we got under way.

As we were gaining speed, my cousin Michael got his boat hook caught in a rope fender hanging from the side of the lock. Michael was still struggling and walking back with the boat hook aft. He did not let go, and the inevitable happened. He stepped off into the swirling water. He could not swim. Although we could swim, we nevertheless shouted 'Man overboard!' Fred, Michael's father, saw him in the water and ran aft, discarding his jacket on the run, and dived into the water. He grabbed hold of Michael as he came to the surface still clutching the boat hook, swam to the side and pushed Michael up an iron ladder on the side of the lock, then followed him up to the top. There was cheering and clapping from the crowd around the lock. I think they thought it was a film set.

We cleared the lock and moored further up the river. Aunt Nance vehemently announced that we were not going any further and we would spend the rest of the holiday exactly where we were. Fred quietly changed his clothes, strung some fishing line from the bow rail to the cockpit and pegged out several wet pound notes, to the merriment of us all.

We started up again after a cup of tea and went through many locks without mishap. It was a memorable holiday.

With some of my school friends, Don, Brian, Lofty, who was very small, and my brother, I went camping at a place near Burnham on Crouch, Maldon on the Blackwater. We paid for the camping site on farmland and had a rowing boat thrown in. The trouble was the extremely fast tides. One day we were out in the boat when the tide changed and was going out, and we could not row back. We were going backwards fast, so we beached the boat a mile away from camp. We had the site for a week and were the only people there. We set up string alarms hung with tin cans, but the only intruder setting off the alarm at night was a dog. We had a great time, but on the Thursday it was cut short. I began to feel quite ill and the train and bus journey home was unpleasant. My school friends also went home. I did not know then what was making me feel so ill, but my mother called a doctor to confirm what she thought – it was chickenpox. My brother got the spots a week later.

Chapter 3

Off to work

(This part is dedicated to Tom Leafe, my friend, workmate and mentor, who should have written this chapter.)

I left school at fifteen to become a Marine Engineer apprentice. I have always loved ships and boats. As I had opted for an engineering bias at technical college it was therefore obvious that I would be destined for the engine room of a ship. This seemed an ideal career for me. I had spent weeks with my father writing letters to various shipbuilders and repairers and graving docks like Green and Silley Weir, Harland and Wolff, The Steam Navigation Company and P&O, all to no avail, as they all had a full complement of apprentices. However one ship-repairing firm, Mills and Knight in Nelson Dock, which had two dry docks in Rotherhithe, had a place for me. It was a couple of bus rides away from Barking. So I went to see Mr Knight for an interview (Mr Mills had died a few years earlier).

I travelled with my father to the dry docks. We got off the bus at Rotherhithe Street close to the Surrey Commercial docks, at the bend of the river between the port and Lime House Reach, which comprises Lavender, Albion, Canada, Quebec, Russia, Greenland and South Docks. The bus stopped almost outside Nelson docks. I noticed the Steam Navigation Co. close by. The wall alongside the pavement where the bus stopped was as high as the bus and consisted of the riveted hull plates of a ship. A wooden fence ran along the top where I saw men in dungarees walking about. I was soon to learn that they were called boiler suits.

We walked to a gap in the wall where there were open wooden and metal gates and a concrete path going up an incline to a stone building, Nelson House. All the other buildings were made of wood and iron and parts of ships. The roofs were corrugated. Everywhere there were chains of all sizes rusting in various heaps with large-toothed cogs. At the end of the dock there was a single wood and iron hand-operated crane. It was Victorian, very Dickensian, although I doubted if I had 'Great Expectations'!

We arrived at the door of Nelson House and rang the bell, and a man in a three-piece suit opened the door. My father said 'We are here to see Mr Knight'. The man nodded and showed us into a large dark room with a huge desk full of papers. There were four heavy leather chairs and a leather swivel chair behind the desk. There were many books on the shelves around the room and as gloomy as it was one could make out pictures and prints of ships on the wall and a portrait of an old gentleman. There were also various lamps, ships' lamps and a large black ornate open fireplace.

At the desk sat a large, red-faced, clean-shaven man who looked well into his sixties or more. He was dressed in a black three-piece suit with gold watch and chain and a white shirt with the old winged collar sporting a grey tie, and had long whitish sideburns. This, with the dark room and old furniture, made me feel that I was indeed in the 1800s.

He got up and said 'Good morning', shook our hands and said 'I'm Mr Knight, you'll be shown around the yard and docks by the gateman you have just seen. Then you will sign the indenture papers for your five-year apprenticeship.' That was all he said at that time.

The gentleman referred to was his accountant, who took us to the offices and the storerooms. The storerooms were negotiated by first climbing down about twenty wooden steps and passing with head bowed through many twists and turns. It was like being in the catacombs. On all sides were shelves with shoebox-sized spaces full of smaller boxes containing screws, nails, nuts, washers, rivets etc. Other areas were devoted to flanges, pipes, all types of rod of various metals and steam valves of various sizes. The storekeeper was about five foot ten, a little taller than my father and me, and had to stoop even more. In one area, the ceiling was a little higher. This was the office, and on the desk many nails had been driven into wooden plaques from underneath, sharp point up. These were festooned with papers, orders for parts and jobs signed by the foreman.

We were then taken around the rest of the yard. The main dry dock, Nelson Dock was about sixty feet deep and stepped on both sides. It was empty of craft and open to the river. The tide was out and one could see the bottom of the dock, where there was a channel. This channel with keel blocks was where the keel of the ship would settle. The small dry dock was built for small tugs and small Danish cargo ships and similar size boats. This was more or less a slipway rather than a dry dock, and ships or boats were drawn up by means of a hydraulic engine with a sort of ratchet with iron rods that were put in and pulled out as the boat progressed slowly up the slipway.

The large dry dock had a caisson that was bowed like the stern of a ship, the bow facing the river. The pressure of the water in the river kept it tight, and when the tide went out so did the water, so timing of the tides was important when accepting a ship into the dock. This dock dated back to the mid-18th century. It was able to take the royal paddle steamers that used to sail from Southend to Calais, the *Daffodil, Monarch* and the *Royal Sovereign;* the latter had apparently left a week before I started. The whole yard seemed quite extensive and also puzzling. There did not seem to be any order, and everywhere parts of machinery were lying around rusting.

After our tour this gentleman bade us goodbye and said we could look around as long as we liked, but to watch our step. He would see us later with Mr Knight back at the office in Nelson House.

My father and I looked around for a few minutes and strolled back to the office. 'What do you think?' said my father a little apprehensively. 'It's OK' I said, 'I think I'll like it'. 'All right' said my father, 'Then let's go and see Mr Knight.'

We walked back into the gloom of Mr Knight's office.

'Well, young sir?' queried Mr Knight.

'Yes, I would like to become an apprentice' I said. He produced papers and my father signed me on for five years as a marine engineer apprentice. Then he shook both our hands and offered my father a dram of whisky, which my father declined. He did not smoke or drink much apart from tea.

'Now' said Mr Knight, 'I want you here at 8.30 am two weeks from now. You will be with three other apprentices. One has almost completed his apprenticeship and the other two have done two years. You finish at 5.30 pm and you will receive one pound, two shillings and eleven pence per week for the first year with an increase each year of fifteen shillings and sixpence. You will also spend every Thursday evening at Poplar Technical College for marine engineering drawing, maths and electrical studies. Also a day release on Wednesday to attend the college.'

We said our goodbyes and left. On the way home by bus my

father said very little except to say I would need a white boiler suit, steel-capped boots, a briefcase for evening classes and my sandwiches.

My mother bought me a steel ruler, a new bomber-type jacket (not leather), a strong pair of corduroy trousers, some shirts and vests. I did not buy a flat cap, even though every person I met at the docks wore one. Only engineers (the fitters) and electricians wore white boiler suits. The rest of the working force, regardless of profession, wore varying shades of blue and black from the oil and grease.

With my gear, I was ready to start work. The two weeks soon passed. My mother was up early in the morning and had prepared a few sandwiches and a florin (two shillings, 20p now) for me to spend on fares and tea. She put them into my new pigskin briefcase. I was a little apprehensive, because I did not think a briefcase was the sort of accoutrement one used at Mills and Knight. I soon only used it when I went to college, although there were never any comments made that I was aware of.

The day came for me to start, and it was 6.30 am when my mother called me to get up. The journey would take about an hour and the buses were usually reliable, but I did not want to be late on my first day. My briefcase was jammed full. It contained my spare shirt and boiler suit. My boots were wrapped in brown paper and tied with string.

I caught the 106 bus from the stop opposite Barking fire station to Canning Town and from there I changed buses for the rest of the journey to Surrey Docks and Rotherhithe Street. The bus was quite full and I sat down on the lower deck with my Aunt Ethel, who had a job in Canning Town. I preferred to sit upstairs with the men and the smoke, and decided the second stage of my journey would be on the top deck. I had not smoked till then apart from the occasional 'drag' at school, but thought I might buy a packet of cigarettes when I got paid.

Although my father regularly gave me between two shillings and half a crown per week pocket money, the thought of my own pay packet was exciting. I would give some of my pay to my mother, as I was now an earner, and we had agreed five shillings a week.

The second leg of the journey was quite different. The bus was full of flat-capped men and upstairs the air was blue with smoke and very warm. The noise of their voices was intermingled with coughing and spitting into their handkerchiefs. The penalty for spitting on the bus was two pounds then. This was the early fifties.

After going through Rotherhithe tunnel we were in the dock area, Rotherhithe Street and Surrey Commercial Docks. This part of the journey was rather slow. We had to wait for a small ship to pass from one dock to another. The road was cut off periodically by a swing bridge which allowed ships to pass through. My excitement was beginning to build, along with some apprehension.

When we arrived I could see crowds of men outside the docks standing in groups. Each group seemed to be headed by a man waving a white card. I found out that these were dockers. They were being picked to work for that day or week for a particular ship or job. I learnt later that it was a closed shop situation whereby the white union cards were passed down from father to son (so I was told). Those that were not picked went home to return the next day.

At this stop the bus almost emptied, the majority of passengers being dockers. Many of them carried, tucked into their belts, vicious-looking hooks with a wooden handle. They were like a foot-long letter J with the top of the J twisted at right angles to the hook. These were for hooking into bales and crates and the netting holding the cargo hanging from the dock cranes. I think they were called baling hooks.

It seemed rather dangerous sitting next to a man with one of these hooks stuck in his belt. Sometimes when a crate was being unloaded there would be a 'mishap' and a load would be broken. The load would more often than not be oranges or bananas or other 'worthwhile' imports. This complicated and hard era of the docker is now gone because of container cargo ships. I feel this was probably accelerated by the dockers' attitudes and the strikes. During my apprenticeship there were a quite a few strikes and troubles in the docks.

The bus stopped in Rotherhithe Street opposite Silver Walk and Acorn Walk. Here there was a shop-cum-café, and it was full of men having their tea and toast and a smoke. I walked towards Nelson Dock opposite Silver walk on the other side of the road, entered the gateway to Mills and Knight and stood by Mr Knight's office. The gentleman I had met on my first visit saw me and beckoned me over. 'Morning son' he said, 'You are to report to Mr George Lewis, your chargehand. You are to clock in. I will give you your card.' He went inside and came out five minutes later with my clocking-in card, my name and number on top. The time clock on the wall would accept my card at 8.30 am and I punched it in.

'Where will I find Mr Lewis?' I asked.

'Follow us' said one of the men. They clocked in and I followed them past a small dry dock that I had noticed on my initial visit and towards the larger Nelson Dock. They turned right into a large wood and metal corrugated building, where they opened a large door. I could not see inside, it was so dark. It took a minute or so for my eyes to be accustomed to the gloom.

After several paces across a wooden floor with various pieces of machinery to my left and right, mainly drills, I reached a wide wooden staircase which led down to a concrete floor about eight feet below. There were three rows of machinery stretching to the end of the 'shop'. They consisted mainly of lathes, some huge, some small, and milling machines. One great lathe was almost the whole length of the floor with a chuck about four to five feet in diameter to take propeller shafts.

We walked towards the end of the building, where there was a large coke-burning stove with a metal chimney going straight up through the roof. I turned left and up another flight of wooden stairs to another floor, wooden and about a quarter the size of the main building. This was covered with drills, metal sawing machines and milling machines. These were driven by their own electric motors, whereas all the other machines were driven by one motor that drove a leather belt that turned wheels to drive all the machines via other leather belts. These came down to the machines from above. The whole roof area was crossed with these belts.

Incidentally, apprentices I met at evening classes told me that all the other shipbuilding firms I had written to had electrically driven machines. This was indeed a Dickensian establishment. Mills and Knight, however, was a ship repairer and not a ship builder. It was also referred to as a 'graving dock'.

I reached a small office near to a door that opened onto the large dry dock. This was the office of the foreman, Mr Tansley. He told me to take a seat and proceeded to tell me what my duties were. He repeated some of the information given me by Mr Knight regarding classes etc. I was to see Mr Lewis.

At that point Mr Lewis came in. 'Morning, Brian isn't it?'

'Yes,' I replied.

'OK, you'll be put with Ron and John, two other apprentices. They'll show you the ropes and tell you what to do. Listen carefully to what everyone tells you. This is a dangerous place with many traps for the uninitiated, so watch your step, OK?'

'Yes sir,' I replied.

'Not sir, laddie,' he said. 'Mr Lewis will do.' He took me to Ron and John, introduced me and left.

'Right,' said John, 'This is where we hang out'. John was about eighteen years old, about my height, five foot eight or nine, and always smoking a cigarette with pursed lips. At the bottom of the stairs from the foreman's office and immediately to the left was a huge milling machine. Judging by the dust and grease, it had not been used for years. The flat milling bed was four to five feet square. It was very dark behind it and difficult to see anything. Behind a table were two wooden benches to sit on, and on the wall three wooden boxes with doors for your gear nailed and screwed to the wall. All the boxes were different, obviously home-made. 'That one's yours,' said Ron. He also smoked, but with the cigarette at the side of his mouth. He was usually smiling and he had a false tooth, which he frequently pushed out with his tongue whilst grinning at you. It had been knocked out in some pub, I was told. We were very secluded, as no one outside could see past the milling machine.

I opened the box on the wall and to my delight it was not quite empty. It had a steel punch and a scribe on the shelf. But I was without tools and was not sure how I was to obtain or borrow them. Ron said he had an old padlock and chain somewhere and if he could find it I could have it.

I took off my bomber-type jacket, removed my shoes and pulled out my white boiler suit. 'Fuckin hell' said John, 'That won't stay like that for five minutes'. His boiler suit was black and shiny with grease. Ron's was not much better, but his was basically a blue suit.

I put on my steel-toecapped boots and was ready. 'Oy Brian!' said Ron, 'You'll need this.' It was a sweat rag to tie around the neck. He rummaged under the steel table and pulled out a flat cap. It looked metallic with the oil and grease in it. 'Try it on' said Ron. I put it on and it fitted. The inside didn't look too bad, Mum could give it a wash. I thanked him.

'Fag?' said John. 'No thanks' I said, 'I don't smoke.' This was not exactly true. I did not swear either in their company because every other word I heard was 'fuck this' or 'fuck that'. However at Poplar Technical College I did both smoke and swear.

It did not take me long to meet the people I was to be with throughout my apprenticeship. Ron and John gave me the history and character, as they saw it, of each person after the introductions. John had steam-scalding scars on his left arm and shoulder. He was undoing a pipe flange that was joined to a boiler outlet pipe. He did not obey the cardinal rule: first you should gently slacken off half the bolts on one side of the flange, so that residual steam is allowed to escape. The steam was under some pressure apparently and forced the two flanges apart. He had undone all the nuts and superheated steam forced the flanges apart and scalded him. He spent two months in hospital and was fighting for compensation.

'Mr Knight you won't see again' said Ron, 'except when he goes home in his chauffeur driven car at about 4.30pm and again when you finish your apprenticeship'. 'Yeah and you won't see much of Tansley either' said John.

Mr Tansley was a tallish man, clean-shaven and a balding head. He wore a flat cap when he left his office.

'George Lewis will be fussing around us all day long, but he's all right' said Ron.

'Jock Thompson is a nice bloke, he don't say much though' said John.

Jock was always dressed in a dark suit with a waistcoat, both dark and shiny with grease, plus a fob watch. He also wore a bowler hat. When a job was given to him he took Soldier Bill, his fitter's mate with him. They were both fiftyish, and Soldier Bill was about six feet tall and large in girth. He always had his boiler suit on. Jock, however, would remove his bowler hat and jacket and pull on his whitish boiler suit over the top. Rarely was he seen without his pipe. He was a short man, about five and a half feet, similar to Mr Lewis. I noticed his left little finger was missing, and he had knobbly arthritic knuckles.

On my first day they had to go to Surrey Docks to repair a piston on a cargo ship, so that week I did not see them after the first day.

Stan Miller was another fitter and his mate was Tom Leafe. Stan was about six foot tall and slim and about twenty-six years old. Tom became a very close friend of mine. He was a writer and wrote short stories. He worked as a fitter's mate to feed and clothe himself and his wife.

In the 'shop', the main building that I entered first, I was introduced to Jack, the 'donkeyman'. The donkeyman on board ship was the man who looked after the engineers' stores. Jack also looked after the coke stove in the middle of the shop floor. He regularly fed coke into the top of the stove, which allowed fumes to escape. Not very healthy! He also made tea in the mornings for the turners on the lathes – there were only two. 'Jack the Donkey' also had a small store. If there were any pieces of equipment not in his store he would make out a 'chitty' and an apprentice would go and fetch it from the main store near Nelson House that I visited on my first day with my father. His main stock consisted of every nut, bolt, screw, nail, die, cutters, shackles and chains etc etc.

Fred Coulson was one of the turners. I got to know him quite well. The other was Ted Trotman.

'You've got to be very patient with Fred' said Ron. 'When you ask him a question he probably won't answer you straight away. He's got a terrible stutter and he's probably working hard forming the word. And for Christ's sake don't try and help him complete the word because if you get it wrong he gets very upset.'

The amazing thing about the stutter was, I soon learnt, that he did not always stutter with the first letter of the word he was trying to form but a completely different letter, for example: 'K---

K---K---K---K Pass me that F—F—F—F hammer or perhaps D-D-D-mmm D—D where's the B—B—B—mmmmm B-B Screwdriver gone'. Sometimes it would take thirty seconds and sometimes a good minute would elapse.

He wore wire-rimmed spectacles on his round, pleasant face and stopped work every fifteen minutes for a 'roll-up', which he made with meticulous care.

The other turner, Ted, was quiet and always greeted you with a smile. He had a thin dark moustache like Errol Flynn and was quite well spoken. I hardly ever heard either of them use a very strong word, unlike the fitters and mates.

On my second day another apprentice, Brian, came in with Ted Trotman and his mate. He was thin with a bushy moustache and spectacles and was on his last year. He was about five foot eleven and wore a brown trilby hat shiny with grease. He smiled at me and said 'Hello, you're the new lad!' Not a question but a statement, and said rather haughtily. I nodded. They had just come back from a job. Brian, Ted and his mate Vic were always together on most jobs and also during tea breaks.

'Those two think they're Bert Einsteins,' said John. He puffed out a cloud of smoke from his pursed lips in their direction. 'Don't let them intimidate you, you know what I mean, don't let them fuck you around.'

As you came through the main door you noticed a little fellow by the drill smoking a cigarette. He had both hands in his pockets. His shiny greasy cap was pulled down over his eyes. His boiler suit was black, not a trace of the original colour could be seen and it was too big for him. He wore small wire-rimmed pebble glasses. He did not move except to puff out a long stream of smoke. He then pinched out the half-smoked cigarette, put it in his mouth and began to chew it.

'Who's that?' I said.

'Er, that's Pictures,' said John. 'He drills flanges. He doesn't say much, he's usually on his own. In fact nobody knows much about him. He's a fitter's mate, don't know how old he is, a bit past it I think.'

'I've never seen him with a fitter,' said Ron.

'Why is he called Pictures?' I said.

'Dunno, perhaps it's his specs.'

Pictures walked away. He shuffled as he walked with a slight sway from left to right.

I spent the rest of the morning watching Fred on the lathe turning a steel rod and putting a thread on it. A two-inch Whitworth thread, he said.

Tea break was announced by the clanging of a ship's bell from the blacksmiths' yard. We all strolled out past the foreman's office, past the carpenter's shop, the 'chippie', along the front high above the road above the ships' plates, past the end of the dry dock and into a shed roofed in tarpaulin. Inside was a table six foot by four, and around three sides excluding the doorway were benches. Above the benches were shelves displaying tin and china mugs. By the end wall there was a small stove alongside which stood a large aluminium canister with spout and lid and wire handle. Ron immediately picked it up and set it on the table, then took out a piece of paper and a pencil stub from his pocket and started taking tea and toast orders.

Jack had toast and wanted salt on his butter. Others had just a couple of rounds of toast as well as tea. Ron collected the pennies to pay for the order and off he went. He had to walk out of the yard across the road to the café at Silver Walk. He came back a few minutes later with the order.

'Tak' heed laddie' said Jock Thompson to me. 'Next week ye're the tea boy. If ye work it reet laddie, ye can make a profit. Ronnie paid fer his sickle [bicycle] out of it.'

In the shack, as they called it, were Jock, Soldier Bill, John,

Ron, Tom and Stan. George the chargehand had tea with the foreman, I believe. Ted Trotman, Vic and the other apprentice, Brian, had their tea somewhere else.

Whilst we were drinking our tea in came two others, Joe Absalom, an old West Indian fitter with whitish balding curly hair, and his mate Jack, a very thin man, almost skeletal and very stern looking. Joe said hello, but Jack did not. I got to know Joe quite well, but he was to retire that year. The apprentices knew Jack as the 'bloody moaner'. He was also the union man.

After about fifteen minutes the bell rang again for the end of the tea break. We walked out. To our left was a long shed without a frontage. This was the toilet. Four feet wide, six feet high and sixteen feet long approximately, it had a long bench with about five holes each a foot in diameter. It was made of oak and was well polished by many bums. Underneath each hole was a bucket with disinfectant, and on the walls nails stabbing old newspapers. These were cleaned out apparently each day by the scalers (more about them later). There were no doors and during my apprenticeship I only used them in an emergency. Usually I went aboard one of the ships we were working on or in a pub or one of the cafés we visited at lunchtimes.

Tom and Stan made their acquaintance and we began talking. I soon began to realise that Tom was intelligent, and I was impressed when he told me he wrote short stories, although I was a little sceptical at first. Stan, a qualified fitter, was also intelligent but very different from Tom.

I told Tom about my hobbies of painting and biology. Painting I had done since the age of about five and I always came top at school. Biology meant pond life, which I studied mainly with the aid of my own microscope, and it was I suppose secondary to art. Tom was very interested, and it started a close association. He loved operas, I loved the classics and we both loved Beniamino Gigli. If anyone said to Tom 'Oh yes, Gigli, he sings like Mario

Lanza', Tom would have a fit. When Gigli came to England, I can't remember exactly when, he sang for those that greeted him on Brighton Station. It was great.

Nothing much happened for me that week. I began to learn my way around the various yards and in particular the main stores. I can only compare them to the catacombs, but it was always a pleasant chore. The storekeepers were very friendly, chatty and helpful.

The following week was completely different. The chargehand, Mr Lewis, shouted from the top of the stairs, 'Stan and Jock, you're off to Surrey Docks. There's a Greek ship for piston repairs and safety valves on the boilers.' This meant of course that Tom and Soldier Bill, their mates, went too. 'Take Ron, John and young Brian with you' he shouted.

This was exciting! I was off on a job.

They collected their gear and loaded it onto an old lorry that was open at the back. The tools were their own personal property, paid for out of their own pockets. I had noticed the lorry on my first visit, but thought it was part of the yard's other discarded bits of machinery.

Tom told me to take my going-home clothes with me because we were not going back to the yard until the jobs were finished. This meant I would go straight to the ship from home in the morning.

'What about clocking in?' I said.

'George will sort that out,' said Tom.

I don't remember who drove us there, probably Mr Knight's chauffeur. On arrival at the dockside I looked up at the ship. It was the closest I had ever been to a large cargo vessel, and I was in awe. It was still unloading crates, of what I could not see.

I was hard on the heels of the others, up the long gangway running parallel to the side of the ship and onto the deck. I followed them along the deck past doors with odd and different smells, oil and rope being the strongest. We reached a metal door with a small round window about head high and entered. An entirely different smell of oil, diesel and hot metal reached my nostrils. We walked along a steel mesh platform and down steel steps. Looking down was a surprise. I could see engine room crew below me and realised how high I was and how big the engine was. To me it was enormous. I had seen the Woolwich ferry engines, all polished brass, but this was much bigger. There were large pistons with metal walkways around them. There was electrical machinery all round the engine room and in a corner one level up was a caged area with shelves and benches: the donkey man's shop.

Stan and Tom were to fit new bearings on a piston and also the propeller shaft connecting flange. This meant the engine had to be turned at times by hand via the huge flywheel. When the camshaft was at full height it could be got at and the bolts removed. Each nut on the bolt was about a foot in diameter. The bottom half of the bearing was tied. and lifted off and a new bearing sheath could be fitted. The top half of the bearing was the same except the cam had to be turned again. When the new bearings were fitted a lead string was placed in the bearings and then tightly bolted back using a large spanner and sledgehammer. The engine was turned and the bearings removed, then the lead was examined and measured using a micrometer where it was flattened. Where it was uneven scrapers were used, something like a large narrow trowel with a hard sharp edge to scrape the soft medal until it was even. The bearings had to be removed several times until it was judged right. The fault had been causing a knocking in the engine.

George Lewis came aboard and took John, Ron and me to a condenser. This was a small boiler about fifteen feet by eight feet in diameter filled with metal tubes and capped at both ends like the main part of a steam locomotive. We removed the two ends, John and I on a plank on one end and similarly Ron on the other. A long rod with a brush on the end, similar to a chimney sweep's brush only narrower and not unlike a bottlebrush, was pushed through the pipes and pulled completely through by Ron, who reversed it and fed it through another pipe. I grabbed the end and pulled it through. I was immediately covered in foul-smelling black and brown rusty-coloured liquid. Was this right? I pushed the rod back through another tube as instructed and Ron pulled from the other side. 'Fuckin' shit' I heard from Ron. We continued in this way, and there were about fifty tubes to do.

We were about half finished before lunch. We stripped off by the chief engineer's office, where there was a cubicle and a hose. We hosed ourselves down and cleaned our boiler suits as well as we could. I wondered what my mother would think when she washed my boiler suit, shirt and vest. I had to carry them home on the bus. I was glad it was not the day for evening classes.

Jock and Soldier Bill were working in a different area, on the boilers. The ship had oil-fired boilers as opposed to coal, so it was cleaner.

I met Tom and Stan and went to a pub for lunch. Ron and John followed us. Although I was only fifteen it seemed in order that I could go to a pub. No one seemed at all concerned, but I was a little apprehensive as I had never been in a pub as a customer before.

Stan sniffed the air. 'Where the bloody hell have you three been?' 'Condenser' said John. 'Oh! Right, never mind,' said Stan. Apparently it was the apprentice's job.

'You look all right, Ron' said Tom. 'Yeah' said Ron. 'I had room to dodge the shit on my side.' He pushed out his false tooth with a grin.

We had pork scratchings and a cheese roll. Tom bought me a half pint of bitter, while they had pints. My drinking in the past had extended to a glass of sherry or Dubonnet at Christmas. The landlady took no notice. I suppose I was as dirty as the other apprentices and with my cap on I looked the same age. I enjoyed the half pint, albeit a little more bitter than I was used to, and I felt grown up.

We finished our job earlier than the others. We cleaned ourselves as well as we could and hung our boiler suits over some hot steam pipes. I climbed down to the engine room floor, where Tom and Stan were working, but they seemed to be packing up for the day.

Suddenly there came a loud shout of 'BELOW!' Tom and Stan crouched and put their hands over their heads. There was a loud clang. It was a two-inch nut that had dropped from where Jock and Soldier Bill were working further along the engine room, nowhere near us. However the reaction was immediate.

The foreman, George, came in and said if we were finished we could 'fuck off home' and added 'Remember the lesson just given you. When you hear 'below' don't look up, cover yourself. If someone's working above you never look up. Got it?'

Hard hats? I don't remember ever seeing one!

I said my goodbyes and left. I had thoroughly enjoyed myself that day, even though I arrived home smelly and dirty. I bought myself a packet of five Woodbines at the shop near Surrey docks for the second half of my journey home.

I went upstairs on the bus, which was fairly full except for my favourite seat right at the back by the window on the left. I sat back and contemplated my day. Ah! I'll have a cigarette – but I had no matches. A man in front of me still wearing his flat cap and smoking a pipe gave me a light. I sat back and smoked, very pleased with myself until I started feeling dizzy. I was smoking too fast. I took it easy and felt at ease with the world.

My parents asked many questions of course, but were pleased because I was pleased.

I gave my mother the agreed amount for housekeeping at the

end of the week and gave a couple of shillings to my brother Peter. He was still at college, the same college as myself, and was into photography. I had enough for the cinema, with change. I got one pound thirteen shillings and sixpence a week. My bus fare was nine pence (about 4 new pence).

Every morning over the next few weeks I would walk into the engineers' shop, glance to my left and say good morning to 'Mr Pictures', receiving a nod, and then I would proceed down the steps, chat patiently to Fred on the first left-hand lathe and then get changed.

One morning I saw 'Pictures' at the drill, drilling holes in a flange plate. I climbed the steps and said 'Hello Mr Pictures'.

'Juz' Pictures' he said gruffly.

'Do you go out on the ships?' I asked. He looked up. His glasses were smeared with grease. His cap peak was almost perched on them. There was a 'dew-drop' on the end of his long nose, black in the pores of the skin. 'No' he said, and spat at the drill bit for lubrication, chewing at his tobacco. The acrid tobacco-stained spit steamed up from the hot drill bit. I decided that I was not going to get any more conversation from him.

George Lewis was another man who lubricated the drill bits with saliva. He showed me how to drill holes in flanges. The holes had to be spaced accurately to fit the bolts. Using a punch, a mark is hammered in the centre of the flange. With a protractor and rule the distances for the holes and the spacing were calculated. Punch marks were made at the measured intervals. A drill bit of the right size for the bolt was fitted in the machine. George showed me that a milky liquid was used for lubrication and cooling the bit, as used on lathes, milling machines etc.

George, who had previously been given a cigarette, removed the tobacco from the rice paper and popped it into his mouth. He pressed the green button and off we went. The bit got hot, the metal spiralling outwards when the drill cut into it. He spat at the bit every few seconds. 'Off you go' he said, handing me the knobbed wheel that pulled the bit down. It was not hard, but I did not spit. He handed me a can of lubricant with a smile.

I was not making much profit from the tea and toast, at least not enough for a bike. It was tuppence a slice for the toast and the same for a 'cuppa'. The change from the café was a halfpenny a cup, and the same for toast.

The lady of the café at Silver Walk was a big buxom woman about thirty years old. Her name was Kathy. The governor, her father, was somewhat hunchbacked and served in the café. She was the cook behind the counter. The apprentices, fitters and their mates regularly made ribald comments. 'She'll 'ave you one day lad. She likes young apprentices!' This gave me little concern, as I did not notice anything that would make me believe them. One day however she gave me a boiled egg with a wink. I pocketed it and thanked her. I was now a little worried, as she was a big woman.

I got back to the shack, distributed the tea and toast, poured out my tea and began shelling my egg. 'How much was the egg?' asked Ron. 'Kathy gave it me' I said. 'Ooooh!' came the chorus from those in the shack. Big smiles and a few 'Hmmms' made me realise I had been set up. I whispered to Tom, 'Did Ron engineer this ?' 'Who else?' he said with a grin. I felt much better.

During my first year I went out on several jobs. One was with Brian, the senior apprentice. He had to replace a broken piston rod from a steam winch that pulled up the anchor. It was a large tug and was moored at the Commercial Docks. It was winter and was very frosty. Brian was quite officious. I think it was his first job on his own.

He got me doing all the work, but I didn't mind, I enjoyed it. He was very watchful, naturally, and vociferous with good information. It took all day. I think he was pleased because the winch started up without mishap the first time of asking. The only problems were the slippery deck and cold fingers. Regular cups of tea supplied by a member of the crew were very acceptable. After that day Brian and I became more talkative and I learnt quite a bit from him, especially about the academic problems I had at evening classes.

Some evenings I did not arrive home until very late. I spent those evenings pleasantly with Tom and his wife at their home in New Cross. When he found out that I painted he asked me to do ten small pictures on plywood that he would prepare, saying he would suggest the subjects. He wanted the first to represent the Big Bang Theory and the rest to depict the stages of the development of the Earth. The last two were to be symbolic representations of the present and the possible future. I finished them in a couple of months and he was satisfied enough to fix them right across one wall of his living room. It apparently provoked much comment and discussion with his family and friends.

Tom let me read some of the short stories he was sending to various magazines. He actually had one read out on the BBC, called 'Compensation Side'. Tom was always complaining about the unimaginative naming of his sisters by his parents. His surname was Leafe and his sisters were named Ivy and Rose. His first name was actually Albert, but he did not like it so he used his second name, Tom. However it was only much later when I wrote him a letter and addressed it that I realised his parents had not forgotten him. I reopened the letter and pointed out his name, A. T. Leafe. He wrote me back shortly afterwards: 'Dear Brian-Bastard! Yours Tom'. He had never noticed the pun on his name and could not believe that his parents had purposely named him thus.

Stan, who was Tom's fitter, was also an intelligent man. He devised and made several pieces of equipment to make the removal of certain valves much easier. One such idea he actually patented. He was always having a go at Tom regarding Tom's philosophy of life.

Tom said to me that he thought Stan was schizophrenic. Stan argued that time and space could not go on forever, ad infinitum. Tom always countered 'OK, put an end to it, build a brick wall around your time and space. What's over the brick wall then?'

On the way back from a café one lunchtime we were walking along the pavement from Rotherhithe Street, where buses regularly passed us. A bus could be heard approaching us from behind. As it passed, Tom gave a shout, I turned around and saw him standing in the road close to the kerb. Puzzled by the shout, but thinking he was going to cross the road, I crossed over. Stan was smiling, Tom was not.

'All right Tom?' I asked.

'No' said Tom, 'but not to worry. I think Stan was trying to tell me that he could kill me if he wanted to.'

'What?' I said, puzzled. Tom just shrugged his shoulders.

Later, one evening at his home, Tom went into great detail about the character of a schizophrenic. He explained that they could be brilliant with much energy some of the time, and go into a deep depression on other occasions. Apart from Stan he thought Pictures was one also. Not that I saw much of Pictures to form an opinion, and anyway at my age it was all a bit bewildering.

During the winter I spent many afternoons in the shop on the lathes with Sid and Fred, more often with Fred. Although it was very difficult being taught by Fred because of his marked stutter, I learnt most of my turning skills from him. He had a great sense of humour, and when telling a joke it became even funnier when eventually he managed to deliver the punchline.

The huge main lathe in the middle of the shop was hardly ever used, but that winter it was cleaned up and made ready. It took all day, with Sid in charge winching with many pulleys, blocks and chains to get a twenty-foot steel rod with a diameter of two feet plus an attached flange lowered onto the bed of the lathe and fitted into the chuck. The donkey man, Jack, was helping and the chain gang was also employed. The chain gang was part of the Blacksmith team. This steel rod was to be turned to the right size and was to be part of a propeller shaft.

The following day with the large belt driving the lathe, it began to turn slowly. A continuous stream of milky coolant-cum-lubricant was pouring onto the cutting tool. It seemed to take ages for the tool to travel from one end of the rod to the other. Sid was at the lathe all day.

The following week I was sent out to accompany Jock Thompson and Soldier Bill, Ted Trotman and his mate Vic. We were to repair the main safety valves on the boiler of a Danish cargo ship. It had just unloaded timber at Surrey Docks and was now berthed at Greenland Dock. The boiler itself was also to be inspected. It was freezing that day, but atop the boiler it was hot. The sweat rags around our necks were useful as the sweat, mixed with thick dust from the boiler top, was running down our faces.

Jock and Soldier Bill removed the safety valves from the top of the boiler and sent them back to the shop. They would be replaced with new ones but would have to be accurately turned on the lathes to the same dimensions as the damaged ones.

Ted and his mate Vic were to inspect the boiler inside and out. To get inside the boiler they loosened the bolts on a small oval plate on top of the boiler, positioned to one side of the safety valves. When the plate was removed it revealed an opening of about two feet by eighteen inches. A knotted rope was tied to a couple of the protruding bolts and thrown down the hole. Ted climbed down and called to Vic. Vic was bigger than Ted and only just squeezed through the opening. He then called me to hand down the hammers, chisels and the electric lamp. This was a light bulb on the end of a cable and protected by a wire cage. To get through the hole you lowered yourself feet first, but then you could only get your shoulders through the hole by raising one arm above your head and then sliding through, using your feet to grip the rope. Once through and standing on the bottom of the boiler I could see the others down the other end and the opening at the top about twelve feet above me. Fortunately I did not suffer from claustrophobia.

Ted began to hammer at the sides, and the noise was terrible. It echoed around the boiler. It was like being inside a huge bell. The heat was oppressive and we were all sweating profusely. Vic was holding the lamp and Ted was chiselling at the sides, removing rust and muck and inspecting the condition of the boiler generally. Normally scalers would be used to do the job, but we were not qualified to inspect.

After about half an hour he seemed satisfied. He then inspected the inlet pipe joints and said we were finished and we could get out. Ted went up first, shinning up the rope, reaching the opening, thrusting one arm up and through, next the shoulder and then pulling the rest of his body through the hole. It was a very tight squeeze. In the heat our bodies had expanded. I found I could not make it and climbed down again. Vic looked concerned. He was about my size, bigger than Ted. He went up, but could not manage it.

'Ted' he shouted, 'We'll 'ave to strip off!'

'Right O' said Ted, not sounding too worried. 'Hand your clothes and the tools up.'

We stripped off to our vests and pants, putting our boots back on again, and handed them up through the hole via the rope. The next thing I noticed was Ted sticking a hose pipe through the hole, which Vic grabbed. 'Right, turn it on,' said Vic. I was puzzled. Vic seemed a little worried – perhaps he was a little claustrophobic.

Then a cold jet of water hit me. I gasped, it was quite a shock to the system. Vic kept it on me for about a minute and then hosed himself. He also gasped. He gave me a grin – a bit of bravado I thought! He called out to Ted, who turned off the hose and pulled it up. Vic went up first very quickly and got through with a squeeze. I followed without any difficulty.

'Well that's an experience for you. You'll probably never have to do that again. I hope you both behaved yourselves in there,' said Ted.

'Bollocks!' said Vic. Apparently we might have managed if we had just removed our boiler suits, but we might have got stuck. Vic and I stood next to the hot steam pipes and dried ourselves with rags. We were soon dry enough to get dressed, although our underwear was still a bit damp.

In the spring a few small ships and boats had come into the dry dock, trawlers and tugs mainly, but I was not called to help on any of the jobs. One week however a big cargo ship was brought into the dock for propeller repairs and for some outer hull plates to be replaced. It had been in a collision and would only just fit into the dock. I was to help George Lewis, Jock Thompson and Soldier Bill to replace the screw (propeller). This would be with the help of the blacksmith and his gang, including the chain gang.

I was quite excited, but the ship was not yet in dock as the shipwrights were waiting for the tide. It would not be high enough until evening, so the shipwrights who would ensure the safe docking of the ship would be working overtime. At high tide tugs would nuzzle the ship into the dock entrance, then winches and ropes pulled by the shipwrights would move it into place. They would then wait for the tide to go out, using shores to keep the ship stable and stop it toppling to one side. Shores are like wooden telegraph poles, although not so thick. As the ship settles with the outgoing tide it is kept from toppling by placing the shores between it and the dockside. The shorter shores go in first and then as the curvature of the ship is exposed the longer ones are used. This involves shipwrights on board and also on the dockside using ropes attached to the shores. The long shores are called 'side shores' and the short ones 'bilge shores'. When the tide is right out the ship will settle on the keel blocks. When this happens the shipwrights hammer wedges between ship and side shores and do the same with the bilge shores to make a tight fit. The ship is now steady and firm.

The following morning as we reached the bus stop outside the dock I could see the ship from the top deck of the bus. The forward masts and funnel could be seen when I got off the bus from the street below. As soon as I had changed into my boiler suit George Lewis called me over and said I was to join him and Jock Thompson. We had to remove the propeller, but had to wait for the shipwrights to erect the scaffolding.

It was a hive of activity. Cylinders of air and oxyacetylene were being placed around the dock. There were cradles dangling from the ship's side, already occupied by riveters and scalers who were scraping away paint and rust from the damaged plates with hand and pneumatic chisels. Electricians were on deck removing lights that had been used during the night's work. Each trade was carrying out its own tasks without overlapping jobs in any way. Breaching this rule, an engineer helping a shipwright or vice versa, for instance, would be frowned upon by the shop stewards. The fitters' shop steward was Jack the moaner. If anyone defaulted in this way there would be a 'down tools' and maybe strike action.

Whilst waiting for the scaffolding to be rigged around the propeller I asked permission to look around the ship and the dock. 'Come back in an hour' said George. 'Don't be late or I'll 'ave your guts for garters.'

Standing at the bottom of the dock and looking up at the ship towering above me was awesome. It could not have compared with a liner or even some of the huge cargo ships, but to me seeing the whole ship was impressive. The propeller blades we had to work on were chipped and pitted, caused I was told by air bubbles. One blade was a little buckled and another had a small crack in it. I walked to the entrance of the dock, stepping between mud and chains lying along the keel blocks. The tide was coming in and a gang of shipwrights were manning the caisson that would close the entrance.

The ship would be slid across the entrance to settle in the silt at the bottom of the dock.

The caisson, pronounced 'casoon' by the fitters, kept the water out when in place by the pressure of the river outside, making a tight seal. The caisson bowed outwards to the river and along the top was a walkway with a chain guardrail on the outer side to prevent anyone falling into the river. However there was none to stop an accidental fall into the dock. The sides of the dry dock were stepped practically the whole length with some gaps allowing iron ladders to the top.

Looking back from the caisson end of the dock to the ship, I could see that the scaffolding was almost finished and George was waving at me. It was time to get back. I climbed the iron ladder to the top and walked along the side of the dock to the scaffolding, then crossed onto the platform via a gangplank with a rope as a banister. I was told to fetch two sledgehammers and then go to the stores and get two iron eyebolts.

On my way to the store I heard a clang and then a loud bang. I stopped and looked over the side of the dock. What looked like an air cylinder had rolled over the edge of the dock and exploded on impact with the dock floor. The metal casing had not broken, but the valve connection had snapped off. It had propelled the cylinder along the floor until it came to rest against the wall. Fortunately no one was hurt, but the language was loud and very fruity.

On the way back I had to pass the blacksmith's shop. This was another busy area with two furnaces roaring. I could see in buckets red-hot rivets obviously for plate repair.

I only just managed to carry the sledgehammers to the platform. I then handed over the eyebolts to be fitted to the propeller cone and then secured with ropes. It was too heavy to manipulate by hand. We also had cylinders of gas and air for burners to heat the cone. Before fitting the eye bolts the burners were switched on and lit with Jock's lighter and then his pipe. George had one burner and I had the other. After about half an hour of heating the cone with the burners they were switched off. Jock hit it with a sledgehammer, but it did not budge. Then both Jock and Soldier Bill hammered away, to loosen up the cone. The eyebolts were screwed into threaded holes in the cone and then ropes were attached through the holes and securely tied to the rudder and the ship's stern. A few more blows and then they began to hammer more on the port side of the cone. I realised then that it must be a left-hand thread.

As the cone turned George told me to step to one side. Jock checked the ropes and gave the cone a blow with the hammer. The cone turned, slid off and swung outwards, banging against the rudder. It was then hauled to the dockside. The uncovered shaft end revealed a nut about two feet in diameter. This also had a left-hand thread.

Burners were again used, but this time a huge spanner tied with ropes was attached to the nut. This was hit with a sledgehammer and the nut began to unscrew. Eyebolts were again used.

During this time Jack the donkeyman arrived and was securing the propeller with the help of – could it be? Yes, it was 'Pictures' leaning over the stern.

'Hello Mr Pictures' I said.

'Juz Pictures' he said, peering over his pebble glasses.

'Ye won't get much more oota him,' said Jock.

With the nut removed and taken away the propeller had to come off next, and was only held on with the key. Where the shaft went through the propeller there was an oblong block of metal cut half into the propeller and half into the shaft. 'What's that Mr Lewis?' I said.

'That, old son, is the key' said Mr Lewis. 'Without that bugger the shaft would go round but the screw wouldn't, would it? This screw weighs a couple of tons or more, so when we've sweated it a bit with the burners we'll clout it with the hammers a couple of times and then stand back and move out the bloody way. You' he said to me, 'Move out now'. I went to the side of the dock.

Jock and George Lewis applied the burners whilst Soldier Bill, who had been standing by at the side of the dock assisting with the cylinders and tools, grabbed hold of the rope holding the propeller and took the strain. Jock then came off the platform and grabbed another rope and told me to pull it as if to stop the propeller coming off the shaft. George then swung the hammer and hit the propeller at the base between the blades or flukes. The propeller slid off. George dropped the hammer. Soldier Bill shouted 'Below!' The propeller swung outwards. I pulled as hard as I could with Jock, but the heavy screw still swung outwards. As if in slow motion I saw George grab hold of the port side fluke as it swung across the platform and collided with the rudder stanchion. If George had not clung to the propeller like a trapeze artist he would have been either crushed against the rudder or knocked off the platform as it swung. With great effort on the ropes, we managed to stop the pendulum swing.

George climbed off, stuffed some tobacco in his mouth, wiped his forehead and with a grin said, 'There must be another way of doing that job but I don't know of one'.

The 'Below' shout had been for the sledgehammer. On its way down it would have done serious damage to anyone if it had made contact. It did however make a mess of one of the fitters' box of tools. Two broken clawhammers, bent feelers and spanners were amongst the splintered wood, but his micrometer was OK.

I spent my lunch times in the shack only when I was working on a ship in the dry dock or in the shop on the lathes. If Tom and Stan were working at the yard I would go with them, occasionally to a pub or café. In the shack I would have bread and cheese washed down with a pint of milk. I rushed my lunch so that I could watch the work on the ship.

Afterwards the propeller was removed and taken dockside. It could not be repaired in the workshop as it was too badly damaged. We waited for the arrival of a new propeller. I stayed around whilst waiting for the new one to arrive so that I could watch the riveters on the cradles attached to the side of the ship at work. They had thick gloves on and held buckets. The red-hot rivets from the blacksmiths' yard were literally thrown using tongs to the riveters, who caught them in the buckets. With tongs the riveters presented the rivet to a prepared hole in the new plate. Inside the ship was another riveter with a hammer. The rivet would then be hammered flat. The rivet was about the same size and shape as a champagne cork. The catching and hammering were very fast. At the same time oxy-acetylene welders were at work.

The ship was in dock for two weeks, and I helped Jock and Soldier Bill with the new propeller. The difference handling the new one was that Jack the donkeyman was the key man, using block and tackle and chains to manoeuvre the propeller accurately. It had to be fitted onto the shaft with the key grooves in alignment. We manhandled the propeller onto the shaft with the aid of the pulleys and then hammered home the key and then the propeller. Next came the nut and then the cone.

During all the activity both inside and outside the ship, there was only one accident that I heard about. One of the fitters was fitting a bearing to the camshaft of number one piston. His mate, who was holding the gunmetal sleeve in place, did not take his little and ring fingers away when the engine was being turned.

The weight of the engine plus the bearing dropped home onto the retaining bolts on the bottom bearing lying above the sump. 'Oh fuck!' he shouted, 'That hurt!' He pulled his hand away, not realising what had happened to his fingers. The fitter saw that his mate was bleeding and was missing two fingers, and shouted to turn the engine to raise the bearings out of the sump area. The fingers were found in the oil in the sump. He was rushed to Poplar Hospital in Mr Knight's car, but they could not save the fingers. They were too badly crushed.

Two months after this accident I spoke to him. 'Hello, everything OK?' I said.

'Not bad' he said. 'I'm working in the stores now, it's a lot easier. I think I prefer it. Do you know' he said, 'I didn't feel much at all, it was more the shock of knowing what had happened. It bloody well hurt when I got to the hospital though, when the feeling came back.'

I forget his name. He was out most of the time on other ships before his accident. He was very philosophical about it. He could use the hand quite well. He said it would be better when the thick bandages were removed.

'Will you be going back as a fitter's mate when the bandages come off?' I said.

'No' he replied. 'I'll stay in the stores where it's cleaner and you 'avn't got George on your back all the time.' George was always looking in at the various jobs being done and sticking his oar in, but then that was his job.

When the work was finished on the ship it left the dry dock at high tide. The caisson was pulled to one side. Water would be allowed into or out of the caisson for buoyancy. As the water rose and the ship became buoyant the shores were pulled away with ropes and tugs took over to take the ship out.

The next couple of months were uneventful, except that one lunchtime John, one of the apprentices, and I walked down

Rotherhithe Street and through the tunnel to a café for some eggs, bacon and chips. The café was long with about ten tables down the right-hand side. On the left was the counter where you ordered and paid for the food. It took up about a quarter of the left-hand side and then more tables. Each accommodated four people. The café was practically full except for three seats half way down the right-hand side. The café was occupied mostly with Maltese seamen from one of the ships in dock, I was told later. I was ordering in front of John and ordered my egg, bacon and chips. I usually did this about once a week for a treat. I stood in front of the counter after paying until my food was ready and then grabbed my knife and fork from a heap of utensils in a box.

I started to walk with my plate towards the table with the three vacant seats when I accidentally knocked a plate nearest my right on the first table. It clattered to the floor, along with the egg and chips on it. The café fell silent.

I put my plate back down on the counter and apologised to the Maltese seaman. 'I'll buy you another one,' I said. I could just about afford another one shilling and sixpence. 'No!' was the reply. 'Yes' I said. 'No' he growled and pulled out a flick knife from his pocket. It went snap. I could not believe it. Two more stood up, 'click, click'. 'Oh Christ!' I thought. I grabbed his chair and backed off, holding it in front of me. He lashed at me. I felt something sticky on my right hand. He had cut my right ring finger palm side from about half way to the tip. I did not feel any pain. This all happened in seconds.

John, who was still waiting for his order, grabbed me and pushed me back. Then he reached over to a shelf by the front lace-curtained window and grabbed a rubber-type plant about three feet high in its pot by the trunk. He swung it at the sailor who had cut me. Unfortunately the proprietor of the café was not a keen horticulturist and probably had not watered the plant for months. The plant pot was left on the shelf and the thing that

John swung at the seaman was a sad-looking tangle of dry roots with very little earth.

He threw it at him anyway, opened the front door and shouted, 'Fuck it, run!' I ran.

We must have run about a quarter of a mile back towards the yard. Whilst running I wrapped a handkerchief around my finger. It was bleeding and throbbing. We reached a pub called the Ship and Something, I forget what, and went in for a beer and a cheese roll between us. We made quite a scene in the pub because we started to laugh about the plant pot incident and were soon choking with laughter, perhaps with relief and a little fear.

Back at the yard John told George. He had a look at the cut on my finger. It was rather deep.

'Ain't too bad lad' he said, 'Probably needs a stitch or two. Come here.' He sat me down, went to the small donkeyman's store and had a word with Jack. He came out with some thread and a flat sailmaker's needle.

'You're not sticking that in me' I said.

'Jock!' he shouted. Jock came down the steps from the foreman's office. 'Jock' he said. 'Squeeze the cut on Brian's finger together while I put in a couple of stitches.'

'That needle's too big.' said Jock. 'Jack the donkeyman's got a wee one that he sews his buttons on with'.

'OK' said George.

'Perhaps I should go to the hospital,' I said.

'Och! Not for a wee scratch like that,' said Jock.

George put two stitches in. It hurt. 'Shouldn't you have boiled the needle first?' I said. I would not have been surprised if he had spat on it, as was his custom whilst drilling.

'Not to worry' he said as he poured methylated spirit on it. I nearly went through the ceiling. 'Christ' I said, eyes watering, but they took little notice.

The cut looked quite neat and the bleeding had stopped.

When I got home that evening my mother, who was a nurse, was horrified and immediately removed the stitches, cleaned the wound with antiseptic and rebandaged it. After a couple of weeks it had healed well without an infection. It was sore but flexible. The cut had not severed anything vital.

By now I was confident around the various yards, shops and departments. On the far side of the dry dock, that is Nelson Dock, were old ships' boilers. These at first appeared as if they had been removed from ships or tugs, lifted out of the way and forgotten.

I was told by Soldier Bill one late afternoon to tell the scalers and Blackie the blacksmith, whose name was Jim, that George Lewis wanted them for a job on a ship berthed at the Commercial Docks. 'They're over by the old boilers' he said.

I wandered across the yard, past the dry dock and the fitters' tea shack and across a grassy slope several yards from the edge of the dock. I stumbled occasionally because in the grass were several bottles. On examination I noticed they were small methylated spirits bottles, some broken and some without labels.

I reached two small boilers, and looked around but could not see anyone. I walked around them and saw another boiler toward the end of the yard perimeter. There was still no one to be seen, so I returned to Soldier Bill. 'I didn't see any scalers, Bill' I said.

'Did you go to the furthest boiler?' he said.

'Yes' I replied.

'Did you go around the back?'

'No' I said.

'Well go around the back'.

I returned and walked around the back of the farthest boiler, which was lying lengthways ninety degrees to the dockside hidden by the other boilers, forming a 'T'. The end of the boiler away from the dockside had a hole cut into it, obviously by oxyacetylene cutters. The hole was half concealed by a steel flange. Smoke was curling out of the hole. I poked my head in. I could not see anything at first, but I could smell the cigarette smoke and also methylated spirit. As my eyes got used to the gloom, I noticed the glimmer of a candle at the back of the boiler. I counted six men sitting around on wooden boxes. No one said anything.

'Er, are you the scalers?' I said.

'Oo wansa know?' someone said.

'George Lewis has a job for you. Tomorrow, Commercial Docks,' I said.

'All right mate, tell 'im we'll be over to see 'im'.

I noticed their faces were dirty, wrinkled and blotchy. One of the faces at the back seemed familiar. I was not sure. It was the pebble glasses and cap low over the eyes. Was it Pictures? I thought I had better not intrude. There were two bottles of meths on the floor. The table had tin mugs and plates amongst old newspapers and unlit candles. 'Fire safety is a little weak' I thought.

I went back to Soldier Bill, who was talking to George. 'I delivered your message,' I said, 'But I didn't know who was in charge. Someone said that they would be over to see you.'

George smiled, nodded and walked off to Mr Tansley's office. Bill told me that the scalers were habitual meths drinkers and he was surprised they weren't all blind.

The 'hideaways' built by some gangs in the yard were fascinating. The shipwrights' shop was next to the blacksmith's and seemed to overlap. Between the blacksmiths' shop and our tea shack was a large box with a tight lid filled with white powder. I had noticed that scalers would fill tins with this powder. On enquiry I found out that they were acetylene lamps used when inside boilers or places where an electric light connection was difficult to locate. The powder was calcium carbide. The tin had a small hole in the lid and water was added to the calcium carbide, which produced a gas. This was acetylene. The small hole allowed the gas to escape, and when lit it burned with a very bright white light, somewhat luminous and smoky.

I was sent over to the blacksmiths' for various eyebolts and pins that were specially made by 'Blackie'. Around the shop were many ships' plates, chains of all sizes and some chain links two to three feet in diameter. There were also parts of boilers, winches, capstans and coils of wire mixed with blocks and tackle.

I searched around the shop by the furnaces but could not find Blackie, or Jim as some fitters called him. I walked around a couple of large anvils and saw one of the blacksmith's mates who was also one of the chain gang. On enquiry he told me that the 'blackie' was in the shipwrights' den. Men in the 'chain gang' deal with blocks and tackle and other lifting gear. I walked into the shipwrights' area and found a pile of ships' plates stacked making a square. The smoke coming from the top of this pile gave the game away. The plates were stacked under the main blacksmiths shop and open on three sides. These eight or nine large ships' plates were welded together. From the outside they appeared stacked in a haphazard way. I could not see any opening. There was a gap however between two plates.

I entered and turned right; two paces and it went left. I was confronted by a curtain. I pulled it back to see a similar scene to the scalers in their discarded boiler, but much more sophisticated. An eight-foot wooden table was surrounded by benches and various chairs. These were covered with cushions shiny with grease. The shelves were neatly stacked with cups and plates like a Welsh dresser. An electric light hung from the centre. A stove was at one end with a chimney rising through the roof. The smoke left the shack via a chimney but was piped over the shop roofing to the furnace chimneys. The smoke I saw was cigarette smoke seeping through a crack in the welded ships' plates.

'Allo! What do you want?' said Blackie. He was a huge man with a black drooping moustache and thick arms, as one would expect, being a blacksmith. He did not wear a hat but a thick wide black belt holding up his trousers.

'George sent me for the bolts and pins' I said.

'OK. Brian isn't it?'

'Yes' I answered.

'Sit yerself down and 'ave a tea.' They poured me out a tea and started talking amongst themselves. Four of them were playing cards. There was money on the table. After about ten minutes the 'Smithy' got up and told me to follow him. We went to the Blacksmiths shop where he gave me a dozen various bolts and pins, still quite warm. I could not lift them all, so I decided to make a couple of journeys. He pointed to a sack barrow. I piled most of the pins and bolts onto the barrow and took them to the engineers' shop. I returned for the rest and saw one of the shipwrights' apprentices that I had noticed in their shack.

'You were privileged' he said.

I asked him what he meant.

'Well normally they makes you wait outside while they 'as their tea' he said. 'Anyways Brian, don't speak about the shack 'cos Knighty and others don't know 'ow to get in though they've been 'ere fer years. Most do, though usually they peer round the first bit and then give up. You follered yer nose all the way. See ya.'

'Bye' I said. I collected the other bolts and pins and left.

During that week I was in pain when I sat down during tea breaks. I had developed a boil on my left buttock. Normally boils amongst fitters and their mates appear on the backs of their necks and forearms caused by sweat and chafing and general lack of hygiene, allowing the old staphylococcus to get in. The carbuncle was very common.

'What's the matter with you Brian?' asked Soldier Bill.

'I've got a boil on my left buttock.' I said.

'Oooh!' said George Lewis sarcastically with his chin in the air. 'On your left buttock eh? Soldier Bill, get a needle, we'll deal with the boil on your fucking arse.'

'Trousers down,' said Soldier Bill'.

'Watch 'im' said Ron, sticking his false tooth out with a grin.

'Don't be bloody stupid Ron' said Soldier Bill.

George put a can of water on the coke stove. It soon boiled. Soldier Bill dipped a sweat rag in the water and applied it several times to the boil. It hurt. I was being scalded, but I tried not to show pain, which was difficult. I was somewhat familiar with the treatment as it was like my mother's technique on our boils during the war. Next a sharp pain with the needle, a squeeze and a plaster slapped on from an old first aid kit in a tin from one of the toolboxes in the donkeyman's store. It felt a lot better. 'Saves messing about with hospitals' said Soldier Bill.

When I got home my mother redressed the wound and said it was OK.

In July of that year I was told to join Joe Absalom, the West Indian fitter, as his mate. He was to strip down and repair a Petters diesel engine that drove a water tender. The tender plied the Thames, taking water to ships and boats. It was about fifty feet long with a beam of about fifteen feet. The holds occupied about two thirds of the forward part of the boat. The engine was behind the wheelhouse, which was covered by two hatches with small glass-filled porthole-type windows. The tender did not enter the small dry dock but was moored outside. When the tide was in you could step down from the dockside to the deck, but when the tide was out and resting on the mud you boarded with the aid of a plank.

I was to be with Joe for about three months. This situation pleased me. Every morning except for my day at college I would go straight to the boat. Joe was a quiet fellow and knew his job.

He was very methodical and explained everything to me as he worked.

The engine had twelve cylinders, revealed when the casing cover was removed. The engine was started by a dynamo but could also be turned manually with a large flywheel. The dynamo would be started first and then when it had generated a sufficient charge you pressed the green button on the engine and with a roar off it went.

Joe's task was to strip the engine down to the crankshaft and check for damage and whether or not it had been buckled. This meant that whatever the problem, new bushes had to be made and aligned. All other parts, pistons and rings etc also had to be checked, and this would incorporate the use of leads and a micrometer, a painstaking job.

Joe was to get a bonus and lots of overtime for this job. He said he would 'see me all right' too. I don't think George liked Joe very much because once or twice a week on this particular project he would turn up and question him about what he had done. I know he was the chargehand, but he did not pay as much attention to other fitters.

Joe was displeased I know, but accepted the situation with only an occasional grumble.

He was the first black person that I had come into close contact with. He told me about life in Trinidad and the other islands and we became quite friendly. Unfortunately he also told me that he would be retiring when this job was finished. He was going back to Trinidad. He was close to sixty years old with his white curly hair.

One afternoon during low tide George shouted from the shore to Joe. Joe went up the short ladder and poked his head out of the engine room hatch. 'When do you think you'll 'av this job finished?' yelled George.

'Probably another couple of weeks more than the schedule. I'm not happy with some of the piston rings.' said Joe.

'Well you've got a deadline. I want this finished and ready for trials by next Wednesday week.' said George. This would give Joe about ten days to finish.

'I'm not goin' to rush this job.' said Joe.

'I said next Wednesday week and that's what I want' said George. 'I'm coming aboard to see what yer problem is.'

'I've told you' said Joe.

'Well I'm still coming aboard to have a look' said George.

George seemed a little annoyed, without reason. He jumped on the plank that went from the shore to the boat. The plank bowed with his weight and then straightened as if he was on a trampoline. It threw George a few inches in the air, causing him to lose his balance. He came down on one foot, toppled sideways and landed on his back in the mud. 'Why didn't you fucking tell me the plank was springy?' shouted George.

What made matters worse was that Joe could not answer him. He was doubled up with laughter and clicking his fingers. I ducked down below, because I was also laughing and I did not want George to see me.

George eased himself out of the mud, swearing continuously. He got himself back on the plank and left, spitting tobacco, at least I think it was tobacco. 'I think I have made a bit of an enemy' said Joe, 'but I don' care. I think he will stay clear for a bit.'

I was at college when Joe finished assembling the engine. However he waited until Thursday before trying so that I would be present. That morning the tide was in and we both went down to the engine room. There was just enough room to walk either side of the engine. The skipper and engineer of the boat turned up with George Lewis. During the three months working on the boat the engineer only visited us on two occasions to check progress. They remained on deck with the hatches open.

Joe started the dynamo and after a couple of minutes he nodded for me to start the engine. I pressed the green button. Nothing happened. Joe went and put a bar in the flywheel and gave it a couple of turns, pulled out the toggle bar and gave me another nod. With a roar the engine started, coughed a bit, spluttered and then roared into life again. There were smiles all round. This did not last long, however. A minute later there was a loud bang. Joe immediately pressed the red stop button.

'What the bloody hell was that?' said George. Joe was silent. He was unscrewing the cowling. 'Brian! Get down here and no one else. There ain't enough room down here.'

When the top was unbolted and lifted off it could be seen that the ring on the aft piston was broken. Joe examined the ring and decided there was a flaw in it. He went on deck and tossed the ring to George and told him he wanted another one today. George did not say a word and left quickly.

The new ring was delivered after the turners had finished with it to be fitted and tested. By now it was time to go home and I had evening classes to go to. Joe said I was not to worry. We would do the trials on Friday at high tide. I was quite looking forward to it.

I have been on one large ship where a huge piston rod more than two feet in diameter had pierced the casing of the engine through the side. It must have been one hell of a bang.

On Friday afternoon the tide was up sufficiently for Joe to start the engine and take the boat for a trial with the boat's crew. The dynamo was started up. I got the nod and pressed the button. No need to turn the flywheel, the engine roared into life straight away. The engine cowling was not on because Joe wanted to check the tappets etc and do the tuning.

After about half an hour the cowling was bolted down. I asked if I could go up on deck and was OK'd by Joe, so I went with the skipper to the small wheelhouse. The hatches were open and we could see Joe and the boat's engineer fussing around the engine. I was sent to let go fore and aft and jump back on board. I went back to the wheelhouse. Joe gave the thumbs up to the skipper and the boat immediately responded to the skipper putting it in gear.

As we pulled away from the dockside I could see George running after the boat waving. 'I think he wants to come for the ride, but he's too late,' said the skipper. We travelled up river towards Tower Bridge. This was a first for me. I had only been on the Thames before on the dredger 'Hopper 14' with my father and on a police launch on the River Roding.

The skipper put the engine through its paces. Full speed, slow, reverse and all went well. We were on the river for about two hours. When we moored back at the dock George was not there. Joe patted me on the back. We tied up and walked back to the shop. Joe and both members of the crew went to the offices to sign the release papers.

George was in the shop. 'Where's Joe?' he said.

'Gone over to the office' I said. He left without a word. He was not a happy chargehand. The turners in the shop however were grinning. Fred said 'D-D-D-D- George doesn't like Joe B-B-B-BB you know.'

'I know, Joe's all right,' I replied. 'P-P-P-P-P- he is' said Fred.

Joe's bonus at the end of the job was £80. Compared to my £1 14s 6d per week it was good money. When he got paid he gave me a ten-shilling note, half a week's pay. I was pleased enough, and even more pleased when he gave me his wooden box with handle and a padlocked half flap lid. I could hardly lift it. 'Dese are all ma tools,' he said, 'I don' need 'em any more. They're yours. Ah hopes they'll do you proud.'

I was overwhelmed. They were lovely tools. External and internal callipers, a micrometer, various feelers, hammers, spanners, screwdrivers, punches etc etc. I thanked him very much. He left at the end of the week.

The week after Joe left, the carpenter's shop burnt down. I was not very surprised. The carpenter's shop adjoined the engineer's shop and was about twenty feet by thirty. It was full of timber poles or shores and planks and had two long benches, one with a circular saw and a bandsaw. There were many shelves laden with tins of paints and varnishes. The floor was always covered in sawdust and the 'chippie' was always smoking and his visitors too. Arc welding was also done close by. However it was probably a cigarette that started it.

Men in the yard quickly got hoses and pumps going plus a chain of buckets, but it could not be saved. Mr Knight was also there, but he did not seem particularly concerned as he stood apart from the men smoking a cigar.

For the next two weeks the chippie and the wheelwrights were hard at work building a new shop, but this time with areas for fire buckets of sand attached to the wall. Fortunately that week there were no ships in dry dock and timber was not required.

For the next month I stayed more or less, apart from errands, in the shop. I was working on the lathes, turning bolts, putting on threads of various Whitworth sizes, putting threads on pipes, filing and making odd spanners to fit certain nuts. I also drilled flanges and milling grooves to fit keys in valves. I did not mind lathe work as it was quite relaxing.

Sometimes the leather belt drive would snap. This meant you had to duck quickly as the belt whipped through the air. The motor would be switched off in the shop and the belt repaired quickly with staples. Sometimes a new strap was fitted.

On the small lathes the cutting tool was moved along manually with the aid of a wheel, but on the large lathes this was done automatically.

A week before Christmas we collected our pay. We would not be back until after Christmas, the day after Boxing Day.

Everyone was pleased on that day because we were being paid an hour earlier. We were paid outside the office and went up to collect our brown pay packets when our names were called. We did not leave the window until we had checked that the amount was right. If not there was a delay until it was sorted out, not without occasional arguments.

Tom, Stan, Ron, John, Jock and I decided to have a drink in the Ship and Anchor, a pub close by. Tom, Stan, Ron and I had a meal of bacon, eggs and chips with bread and butter first at the café across the road, so Jock and John were already in the pub when we arrived. It was packed. There were no seats left and hardly a gap at the bar. Jock was at the bar however and he bought us all a round of drinks. We had to stand near the door. The pub was filled mainly with crew from the ships docked at the Steam Navigation Company's wharf and also from Shaw, Saville and Albion Line ships in the Surrey Docks, London Graving Docks and Orchard Dock.

Standing at the bar close to Jock, who looked smart in his bowler hat and with his watch and chain looped into his waistcoat pockets, was another Scot about the same size as Jock, about five feet five inches. Next to him was a stoker who was about six feet six inches tall and seemed almost as wide across the shoulders. He wore only a flat cap and a sleeveless woolly jumper tucked into black corduroy trousers, and round his neck his sweat rag. He said something to the Scot next to Jock, who shook his head. The stoker, who was not English but I thought Scandinavian, said 'Why you not want a drink with me? It is Christmas!'

'Aim gaen hame noo' said the Scot. 'You not' said the stoker 'until you drink my health with a vodka.'

'All right' said the Scot, 'but I'll have a whisky.'

'What is wrong with vodka?' said the stoker.

'I dinna care for it' said the Scot.

'You vill drink a vodka with me' said the stoker.

By this time the pub was beginning to thin out, not unlike a John Wayne Western.

'No thanks' said the Scot. With this the stoker grabbed the Scot by the lapels of his coat and hit him full in the face with his huge fist. The Scot's face had been flattened – it was a mess. The drunken stoker downed his vodka and stepped over the bleeding and barely conscious Scot. The sound of breaking glass as a bottle crashed onto the stoker's head decided Tom, Stan, Jock, Ron, John and me that it was time to leave. What happened to the Scot and the stoker and the end result of the fracas I never found out, except that we heard the police car bells ringing.

It is amazing how during a bar fight in a John Wayne film the combatants only have a cut lip, a black eye or a bloody nose from full, bloodied punches. In reality just one hard bare-knuckled punch in the face would smash it terribly.

On returning to work after Christmas, Stan and Tom were sent to the East India Docks to repair a bilge pump. I was told to collect the faulty valve so that the turners on the lathe could remove the pitting on the seat of the valve that had caused the leakage.

'Brian! Get your boiler suit off. Go down to the office and collect your fare money. The valve is on a Greek ship. Bring it back as quick as you can. The ship is leaving tomorrow,' said George.

I changed, collected my fare money and my chitty to allow me through the gates and also into the East India docks. Ted collared me and said 'Why don't you use my bike and pocket the fare?' 'Mmm OK,' I replied. The bike was a drop-handled one with a saddlebag and toe clips on the pedals. It also had a fixed wheel. I had never ridden a fixed wheel bike before.

I set off. All went well until I got to Rotherhithe Tunnel. There was a hold up, so I applied my brakes and stopped pedalling. The bike did not free wheel. I was catapulted off the saddle onto the handlebars. The toe clips stopped me going any further. I was a little shaken, but there was no damage done.

I started off again on the road to the docks. There were still tram rails in the cobbled roads. The trams had only recently stopped running and I found out that one should cross them on a bike at approximately at right angles. This I did not do and the front wheel dropped into the iron gap. This time I came off the bike completely. It took a hard pull to extricate the wheel. It was slightly buckled, but I managed to straighten it with my boot.

I set off again without incident. I reached the dock, parked the bike and climbed up the gangway. The gangway ran parallel and diagonally upwards to the ship's side reaching the top deck. I reached the deck and found the iron door to the engine room. The engine room was large and the bottom was a long way down. I started to climb down to the bilge area, where the pump was, negotiating three flights of metal steps.

When I reached the engine room floor, Tom saw me and called out. I went over to them and Stan gave me the faulty valve. 'There's nothing for us to do until you return,' he said. 'We'll have lunch and be back about 2.30, OK?' I nodded. 'Off you go then. How did you get here? By bus?'

'No I used Ted's bike.' I told them I was not used to the fixed wheel and about my mishaps on the way to the docks. 'But I'm all right now,' I said.

I took the valve, which was about four inches in diameter and four inches in height, and climbed back up to the deck into the fresh air. I made my way to the gangway and started to descend. I had not gone more than ten steps when my boot slipped. I hung onto the rail, but the valve jolted out of my hand. I saw it bounce down the steps and then stop. I rushed down towards it, but it was lying on its side rocking in a half circle and then rolled off the gangway into the dock between dock and ship with a plop.

I was in shock. 'Aaaah shit!' I mouthed through clenched teeth. What to do? Do I go back and tell Tom and Stan? I could not bring myself to do this. My mind started racing. Without another thought I cycled back to the shipyard. I wheeled the bike into the shop.

'Right' said George. 'Where's the valve?'

'In the saddlebag,' I replied.

He opened the bag. 'Not bloody well in here,' he said.

'What? It must be' I replied.

'Well it ain't' said George.

'Bloody hell, it must have been when I fell off the bike. The wheel got stuck in the tramway rail,' I said hesitantly.

'Well go back and fucking well look for it!' said George, glaring at me. I went back out and came back about forty-five minutes later.

'Sorry Mr Lewis I can't find it,' I said.

'Jesus Christ,' George said very quietly. Then he loudly told me to go back to the ship and tell Stan what the problem is and to take measurements of the casing. I did so but did not say what had really happened. I was too embarrassed.

They took careful measurements and wrote them down and sent me back again. I was getting quite used to the bike by now. I then collected a new valve from the stores at another shipyard, as we did not have the right size in our storeroom. I brought it back and gave it to Fred the turner. He set up the lathe and turned the valve seating to the required measurements. This took over an hour, but I was soon on my way back to the ship with the valve in the saddlebag.

My journey this time was uneventful. I climbed the gangway clutching the valve tightly in my hand and with relief delivered it to Stan and Tom. I don't think they were too concerned because it meant overtime to get the pump functional before the ship sailed. I went home after returning the bike to Ted. I was emotionally drained, but very relieved that all had turned out well, although I felt somewhat guilty.

The incident cropped up from time to time with the other apprentices in fun, but I never told them the truth and Stan and Tom seemed not to notice that it was a different valve.

Chapter 4

My mother

Soon after the war, my mother Louise began to get restless, so she started work. Her first job was with the Barking Brassware factory in River Road. On the other side of the road was the ACME chimney, made of metal during the war but soon after was demolished and a brick chimney was built with the word ACME in white reading vertically down the stack. I have mentioned this chimney–stack as it was then a landmark.

I saw my mother occasionally at work. She had to make plaster casts for bathroom taps, put them in boxes and fill the moulds with sand ready for molten brass to be poured in. The result was a brass bathroom tap that had to be polished smooth and then chromium plated.

She soon gave up that job and decided to become a nursing orderly. Being ambitious, she then decided to train to become a nurse. She passed her exams with help from my father, who tested her from her medical books. She started work at Poplar Hospital and became friendly with a young ward sister who gave her much help. Her name was Olwen, and she was the woman I later married.

My mother then went into midwifery and again passed her exams. She became friendly with a Trinidadian midwife named Sybil, and when Sybil went back to Trinidad my mother went too. My father had no say in the matter. They were there for over a year, with my father helping by buying, at my mother's request, underwear from Marks and Spencer and posting it off to Trinidad.

Sybil's husband Denis worked in the Pathology Department at East Ham Memorial Hospital, and my mother came back home and worked there. At this time I started work in pathology and soon after my mother left for Auckland, New Zealand. She had passed her Health Visitor's examination and found her role in life looking after the health of the Maoris. She sent for my father, who obediently followed, and then a month or two later my brother and other relatives also went to New Zealand and became naturalised Kiwis.

I stayed behind because I had exams to take and a new baby daughter Bronwen. This was after my demob from the RAMC. Before my parents died, I was able to visit them in New Zealand three times.

Chapter 5

Farewell to the docks

Although I did many interesting and exciting jobs during my apprenticeship, after two years the novelty was beginning to wear off. I was a little concerned when at my evening classes, especially during marine engineering drawing lessons, my drawings were always handed in to the teachers smudged with oil and grease, because I could not wash properly at the shipyard. At first I thought that this was the norm, but apprentices from other shipbuilding firms did not have dirty classwork. I found out about their lathes and the facilities they had. Mills and Knight and Nelson Dock Graving Yard were indeed Dickensian.

I did well at classes however, passing my engineer's drawing examination for the chief engineer's ticket second class, albeit with dirty papers. But I was beginning to be a little concerned about my future as a marine engineer. I was no longer entirely convinced that it was the life for me.

These misgivings were put to one side during a two-week period when an old Royal Navy corvette came into the dry dock for rudder repairs. Whether the ship still belonged to the

Navy was doubtful. It was in need of paint and the small gun amidships looked very rusty. Corvettes were usually named after flowers, but there was no sign of its name. If it belonged to the Navy I'm sure they would have done the job themselves, but I never found out.

I was not involved with this job, but as there was little else for me to do in the shop I asked George if I could go aboard. He went to the foreman, who gave permission provided of course that the captain of the corvette agreed. There was no problem. John and Ron were working on the rudder with Jock Thompson and Soldier Bill. Apparently the connecting rods to the steering gear were broken, so work had to be carried out both inside and outside the ship and scaffolding similar to that used for the propeller removal was constructed.

I went aboard and was allowed to roam around the engine room. I then asked permission to go to the bridge, which was granted. Being on deck, especially on the bridge, was another way of life. I was beginning to realise that being an engineer on board ship did not allow you to see much of the world outside the engine room. You had to love engines. I was not sure I did, to that extent.

When the ship was ready to leave Ron, John, Jock and Soldier Bill were to go along with it for rudder trials when the release papers were signed. Happily I was given permission to go along too. We steamed down the Thames towards Gravesend and Tilbury and out into the Channel. It was a great thrill. I was not allowed on the bridge unfortunately, but I wandered around the deck with the crew around the small gun and aft where there were the remains of the depth charge racks and other small gun emplacements.

When we were well out in the Channel, Jock called for me to come below. 'We're soon to start the trials, laddie. You're to stay here with us. The ship will be going full steam ahead and after about half an hour the bridge will ring down to stand by. So when that happens laddie, hang onto the steps tight. Now go with John and Ron and help the others clear away any loose nuts and bolts and gi 'em to the donkeyman.'

This we did as quickly as we could. It was only about five minutes later when the skipper signalled down to stand by. We all held on. The engine was pounding away noisily. You had to shout to make yourself heard.

Suddenly the ship lurched and began to go over to one side. I was a little worried until I saw Jock, who appeared unconcerned. The skipper had swung the wheel completely over and the momentum of the ship at full speed had turned it like a car on two wheels. The strain on the rudder must have been enormous. There were many clanging noises as pieces of metal and tools that we had not seen and picked up fell from various parts of the engine room. No one was hit, however. I realised that as the ship turned we must have keeled over practically ninety degrees and wondered what it must have been like on deck. This was done four times and then we steamed back to Nelson Dock.

I enjoyed that day and also another day similar but on an ocean-going tug. It was the same team and the same rudder trials but the sea was too rough to stay out long. This time I was allowed out on deck. The tug really hit the waves and they came over the bow up to the bridge house. It was quite impressive. The power of the engines on the tug and the way she ploughed through the waves brought to mind the exploits of a tug in a book I read by Jan de Hartog called 'Captain Jan', salvaging by pulling large ships through rough seas across the Atlantic.

My brother, who had taken photography as his career, was leaving college. He had stayed on an extra year. My mother came home from the hospital where she worked as a nurse one evening and told him there was a vacancy in the Pathology Laboratory for a junior technician working mainly in the microbiology department. 'I thought you would like to go for an interview,' she said. 'No thanks, photography or nothing,' replied my brother.

After about two minutes I said 'Mum, I'll go for the interview.'

'What?' she said, 'But you've already got a job.'

'I know mum but I think a job in the laboratory is more to my liking. You know I've always been interested in pond life and microscopy and I've been having doubts about being a marine engineer.'

'Are you sure?' she said. I nodded.

'Very well, we'd better wait until your father comes home'.

A few months earlier I had taken an examination, with my brother, for a job in the aircraft industry. It was held in the London and there were hundreds of candidates. I took it because of my doubts about marine engineering. My brother, however, was looking for a job. He failed the examination but I passed. Ironically I had no intention of going any further.

After my evening meal my mother told my father my intentions. He shook his head. 'I don't think you can break your apprenticeship as easy as that,' he said. 'Well' I replied, 'I haven't been for the interview yet. Let's wait and see'.

I went for the interview at the hospital on a Saturday morning with my mother. I chatted with the pathologist, Dr Ross, for about half an hour. He asked me why I wanted to work in the laboratory, and I told him about my interest in biology. He seemed satisfied and asked me when I could start. I had to tell him I was already apprenticed. He puffed on his pipe and raised his eyebrows. He said if I could get away I could start in two weeks. He then introduced me to one of the white-coated staff and left.

I was shown around the laboratory and was very impressed. I made my mind up – this was what I wanted. I now had two jobs. I told my mother, and when we got home she told my father. 'Are you really certain about this?' said my father. 'Definitely,' I replied. 'OK' he said 'I will write to Mr Knight.'

I went to work as usual on Monday and told Tom about it. He agreed with me that it was the right thing to do and seemed pleased. 'As long as you still spend some weekends with us,' he said. 'Of course, no problem,' I replied. This made me happier.

The following weekend my father received a reply from Mr Knight asking to see my father and me on Monday if it was convenient. My father was doing a night shift, so it was all right with him. I was apprehensive but determined.

We arrived at Mr Knight's large and dismal office at Nelson House on the Monday morning. It was only the second time I had been in the room, the first having been when I was interviewed for my apprenticeship.

Mr Knight was standing behind his desk. 'Well?' he boomed. No other greeting was given. 'You've only been with us for two years and you've three to go. It can't be done. You are articled, and to break this contract will cost you fifty pounds.'

Fifty pounds was a lot of money in the fifties. My father looked concerned. I knew he would get the money for me, but I just could not let him do it. 'All right' I said, 'I'll continue.'

'Right' said Mr Knight.

'But' I interjected loudly, 'For the next three years you will not get a stroke of work out of me.'

There was silence for about a minute, Mr Knight staring at me all the while. In a quiet voice he said. 'If that's the fucking way of it boy then you can piss off.' He picked up my papers from the desk and tore them in shreds. Then he sat down at his desk, turned away from us in his leather swivel chair and picked up his telephone, waving his arm at us to leave. We left.

I went back to the shop whilst my father waited outside in the yard. I was collecting my bits and pieces, a few tools that I wanted and some clothing. I said goodbye to the people in the shop, telling them I would come by and see them tomorrow. On my way out I was stopped by the secretary, who told me to pick up my severance papers and any monies owing me, which I did not think I had. As apprentices we did not get paid overtime. This fitted well with my plans to say goodbye to everyone.

On the bus home my father said, 'That went more smoothly than I thought, are you happy about it?'

'Yes' I replied. I was very happy about it.

The following morning I spent the day saying goodbye. They were all a little surprised at my leaving. Fred said a long and fond farewell: 'T-T-T-T-T Good N-N-N-N-N-N-N-N Bye'. George wished me well. I think he genuinely was not happy about me leaving. I arranged with Tom, Stan, Ron, John, Jock and Soldier Bill to meet at the pub for a drink.

On my way out after saying my goodbyes to the Shipwrights' and Blacksmiths' crew I noticed Pictures by the drilling machine in the engineers' shop. He was looking at me and chewing, probably part of a cigarette. He spat a brown tobacco stream to one side. I could not see his eyes through his wire-rimmed pebble glasses. They were covered in oil and grease. He shuffled a couple of paces towards me and stuck out his oily hand. He pulled it back, wiped it with his sweat rag and offered it again. I took it and shook his hand. 'Cheerio Pictures' I said. He nodded, went inside the shop and began drilling holes in a flange. His lips pursed as he prepared to lubricate the drill bit in the usual way.

Chapter 6

A job in the lab

Queen Mary's Hospital, Stratford

My first day at the hospital in the Pathology Laboratory was rather strange, being a complete contrast to Marine Engineering. I was given a white coat and told what not to touch and about the dangers lurking on certain benches, in particular the bacteriology bench. The chief technician was a Mr Cooling, who chain-smoked cigarettes.

Although primitive to the laboratories of today which have auto analysers, automatic staining machines, blood culture machines and machines doing hundreds of biochemical tests on hundreds of patients per day, carbon dioxide and anaerobic incubators in microbiology departments etc etc, the microbiology or bacteriology department was still basically the same as today. Today health and safety procedures are paramount, not so in those early days.

I started work as a junior medical laboratory technician. Today they are known as medical scientific officers. Although nervous, I was in awe of the many binocular microscopes in the laboratory. However my duties were not very scientific to start with. I washed bottles, cleaned microscope slides, sterilised syringes and instruments and sharpened needles for venepuncture (blood taking) for testing haemoglobin and red and white cell counts. I also made up various batches of culture media for growing bacteria in petri dishes and bottles.

After a couple of months I was allowed to sit at the benches to examine carbol fuchsin stained slides of sputum for Mycobacterium tuberculosis under the microscope. This was a weekly chore done by all the technology staff. Tuberculosis clinics and hospitals were very busy in those days. Patients came in daily with their pots of sputum. Some patients however were a little careless with the screw caps on the pots and started to empty their pockets of sputum onto the tray provided with their hands, which was a little unsavoury to say the least.

My first attempt at blood taking was a very nervous affair. The patient fortunately had good veins when the tourniquet was applied and I was successful. Although I was supervised my hands still shook, but I managed to obtain blood from the vein without causing any distress to the patient and without going right through the vein and causing a bruise. I felt great and never looked back, becoming very proficient even with some of the most awkward veins, those that were deep under layers of fat and those that were so thin as to be very little bigger than the needle.

Some needles became damaged during preparation even though protected by a glass tube. The point of the fine sharp tip sometimes got 'tapped', which caused an invisible hook. Although the needle entered the vein quite well it was difficult to fish out, causing much discomfort. Today of course disposable needles are used and are practically painless.

When I had gained sufficient confidence I was left on my own to bleed patients from the vein and also from the finger using a Hagedorn needle kept in a tube containing spirit with a cork stopper. The blood from the pricked finger was sucked up into a glass graduated tube attached to a rubber tube and the blood then blown into a tube of diluting fluid for haemoglobin estimation and into a graduated bulbous tube mixed with acetic acid and methylene blue for white cell counts and red cell counts. Occasionally pipetting went a little wrong and technicians sucked blood into their mouths. In those days we just spat it out and rinsed. No thoughts about hepatitis etc. Today in the biochemistry departments tests for sodium, potassium and chloride levels in blood are estimated using machines. In the early days of my laboratory work before flame photometers tests were carried out with tedious extraction and measurement of the intensity of colour production with colorimeters. Blood urea estimation took days to extract, and making the appropriate reagents to do the tests sometimes took a week.

Carbon dioxide analysis of the blood using Van Slykes apparatus sometimes involved handling mercury without rubber gloves. This reminded me of my first encounter with mercury. At college my first chemistry lesson given by Mr B., who had a deep slow theatrical voice, dramatically proclaimed whilst holding a large stone jar of mercury, 'Mercury – is – very – heavy'. As he spoke the jar slipped from his grasp and smashed on the floor, the mercury running everywhere and living up to its name of quicksilver. We spent the whole lesson trying to contain our laughter whilst scooping it up with our hands and putting it into another container. I thought it was hilarious, but it was very embarrassing to Mr B.

Len, our biochemist, seemed always in the process of estimating faecal fat content. He could be seen quite often with a pestle and mortar grinding up an oven-dried faecal specimen in preparation for extraction of the fats with alcohol, and at the same time he would reach into his white coat pocket, break off a square of chocolate and pop it into his mouth, while chatting to a colleague at the bench.

Although there were ward rounds for blood-taking, patients who were able would come to the laboratory. In those days all the laboratory disciplines were under the same roof, unlike the specialised departments of today. A 'Lab Tech' had to know Haematology, Biochemistry, Histology and Bacteriology. Now one can obtain a degree in Biomedical sciences and then specialise. Histology split into Histology and Cytology, Microbiology split into Parasitology and Virology. Haematology included blood transfusion techniques.

One day a patient came into the blood-taking room from the wards in her dressing gown, a young dark-haired girl. I say young, although I was not yet eighteen. She sat down and I asked her to roll up her sleeve, but it was too tight. I asked her to remove her dressing gown. I turned around and prepared the syringe. When I turned back again she was completely naked. I was taken completely and embarrassingly by surprise. I told her to replace her gown and went blushing to get a female Lab Tech to do the venepuncture. I do remember she was beautiful and quite unabashed.

Very little shocks me now, although on one occasion I was surprised, but with an effort I managed not to show it. I was doing a skin scrape for ringworm fungus of the scalp. The girl, when I approached her with a scalpel, immediately grabbed hold of her hair and removed it. She was completely bald. It was quite a shock, and the scalp was very much infected. Probably it was the cause of her alopecia, because the microscopy showed many fungal threads.

In the Histology department we dealt with parts of the body removed in the operating theatre. They were processed for microscopic examination to determine whether the piece of tissue was malignant or benign and whether or not it was infected. This was also done with post mortems and came under the classification of morbid anatomy.

Once every so often these specimens had to be disposed of by incineration. One day the chief told me and another junior technician to collect the buckets of formaldehyde containing the tissue and other specimens and take them to the incinerator. One specimen was too large to be carried in a bucket – it was an amputated leg. So it was wrapped in cloth and I had to carry it over my shoulder like a rifle with a bucket in my left hand.

The other technician had just been demobbed from the army and had finished his two years' National Service in the Royal Army Medical Corps. He carried two buckets. We had to walk through the busy Out Patients' Department filled on both sides of the aisle with seated patients. The incinerator was outside the hospital near the Engineers' department.

Halfway down the aisle the wrapping came off the leg, exposing the foot. I had not noticed, but I was aware of screams and other noises and scraping of chairs and general agitation. I turned around and noticed the exposed foot and quickened my pace towards the door. We got to the incinerator, opened the fire door and threw the specimens, including the leg, into the furnace, then closed the fire door. We then walked back to be met by our pathologist and chief technician, who took us aside and gave us a lecture about being more careful in future.

The chief was a stern man but fair. Mr Frank C. chain smoked even whilst investigating and culturing bacteria, using the bench as an ashtray to put his cigarette butt down. Attitudes now have certainly changed, but we were aware of our limitations and appreciated the need for strict adherence to techniques and the necessity of double checking our observations. I was told he developed tests and diagnostic techniques for many diseases in the early days.

I bumped my head on a fridge door one day, on the place

where I had an adolescent spot just above my left eyebrow. The following day my eye was almost closed due to the swelling, with a large yellow pustule. That evening I reported it to the chief, who told me to bathe it in saline and first thing in the morning he would take a specimen of the pus to culture it for Staphylococcus aureus and determine what it was sensitive to. For some reason I decided to go to casualty first thing. They cleaned the swelling, removed the pus and slapped some gauze over my forehead. When the chief saw this he went mad. He grabbed me, clipped me round the ear, sat me down at his bench and unceremoniously whipped the dressing off. Then he swabbed the infected area with ether, still smoking his cigarette, and rammed a wire culture loop into the now cleaned-out hole in my forehead and plated out what little he got on the loop onto an agar petri dish.

'Don't bloody well have anything done in future Brian until you culture it. Understand?'

'Yes' I replied meekly.

Dr Ross was our pathologist. He was never seen without a smoking pipe in his mouth. During our tea breaks we used to retire to the wash-up department amongst the autoclaves and sterilising ovens. Water fights occasionally ensued using large glass 50cc syringes. The water was squirted across the room to those sitting opposite and vice versa. On one occasion water jets were flying back and forth across the room and Dr Ross, oblivious to what was going on, was striding through the room from his office to the main laboratory. A jet of water struck his smoking pipe and there was a hiss of steam. A loud crack was heard and a piece of the pipe broke off. Without altering his stride he looked at what was left of his pipe, murmured 'Hmmm' and carried on. We looked at each other in silence and scattered to our various departments.

After a few months working in the laboratory I used to accompany Don, the demobbed RAMC technician, around the wards to collect blood specimens. One day we had to go to the children's ward to bleed a baby from the heel to do a white cell count and haemoglobin. The iron cot had sides that could be lowered to get to the patient. The day we went was matron's inspection day and all the floors were especially polished and the staff ready for her arrival with the retinue of consultants and registrars.

We collected the blood without any fuss from the baby and raised back one of the cot sides. My side was stuck and I could not raise it. I gave a heave and it came up with a crash. A bucket full of disinfectant and dirty smelly nappies had snagged the cot side. The contents shot across the floor and over Don's shoes. At that moment the matron arrived. The look of horror from the nurses was accompanied by the matron's voice. 'What are those two doing in here?' We helped to clear up the mess and found out later that it had been reported to our pathologist, who spoke to us about it with a smile on his face as he puffed away at his pipe. 'Next time you go to collect blood make sure that matron is not expected,' he said.

In those days everyone wore white coats which were starched stiff. We had a clean one every week unless it became too soiled. It was quite a struggle getting one's arms into the starched sleeves. Everyone had to wear a tie, even with the risk of the ties getting contaminated from the benches etc. I therefore wore a bow tie.

Christmas time was party time. All departments had a party of one sort or another. Don and I, whilst finishing a ward round, were asked to help carry a Christmas tree to a ward on the top floor by the sister. It meant taking it up the stairs that spiralled around the lift shaft. It would not go in the lift. The tree was already festooned with glass balls and tinsel. By the time we got it to the top of the stairs most of the balls had fallen off and crashed down the stairs. At this point we developed a fit of giggles and the tree got away from us and slid halfway back down the stairs.

By the time we got it back up again and to the ward it had lost its splendour. However the sister saw the humour of it as we were both covered in needles, bits of tinsel and glass.

In the large Out-Patients' Department the staff held a Nativity play. The performers were nurses and midwives, and the majority were Irish. Staff and patients were allowed to attend the evening performance. The stage was built using wooden planks nailed to wooden orange boxes with two poles at the front corners joined at the top with ropes and pulleys to hold the curtains. The curtains swooshed back and forth quite well. The carpenters had done a good job.

It was at the point where the Wise Men saw the bright star from the east that the trouble began. One of the Wise Men, an Irish nurse said, 'Behold a stur from ta heast travelling across the skoy'. Then a nurse at the side of the stage pulled a rope to pull the large silver painted star across from one side of the stage to the other. Nothing happened. It just jerked and bobbled on the rope. The Wise Man said again 'Behold a stur from ta heast travelling across t'skoy'. The rope was tugged again, this time with much more vigour, unfortunately too much vigour. The two poles fell in towards each other, carrying the curtains with them. At this point Don, my brother and I stuffed handkerchiefs in our mouths to stifle our laughs, but it was too much. With a triple roar we exploded and quickly left the department. We fell about outside in pain with unsuppressed laughter. On the way home if any one of us started the conversation with 'Behold' we doubled up again. We got home exhausted. I never found out whether the play finished or not.

View from front door of 25 Craven Gardens just after the war

View from my bedroom window just after the war. Fourth house
still shows an air raid shelter

Myself around age 4 and Peter at Laindon with our
red wellies and outfits knitted by Mum

High tea. From left, a friend, Grandmother Anne Styles, Uncle Fred, Uncle Snowie,
Aunt Ethel, my mother Louise and my father George.

Westbury School Barking football team (cup runners up)
Teachers L-R Mr Cox and Mr Coe. I am 5th Left back row

Westbury School Cricket team (champions). Teachers L-R Mr Andrews, Mr Cox and physics master. I am 3rd Left and Fred Rumsey 5th Left middle row.

VE Street party

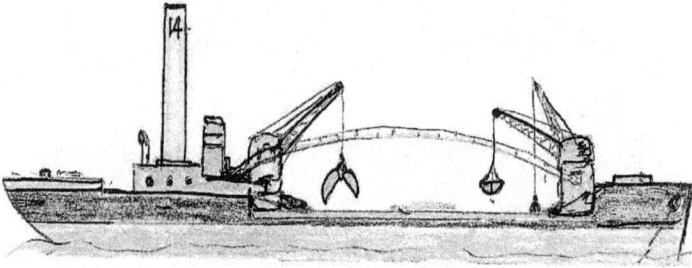

Port of London Authority ''Hopper 14'' Dredger. (Drawn from Memory)

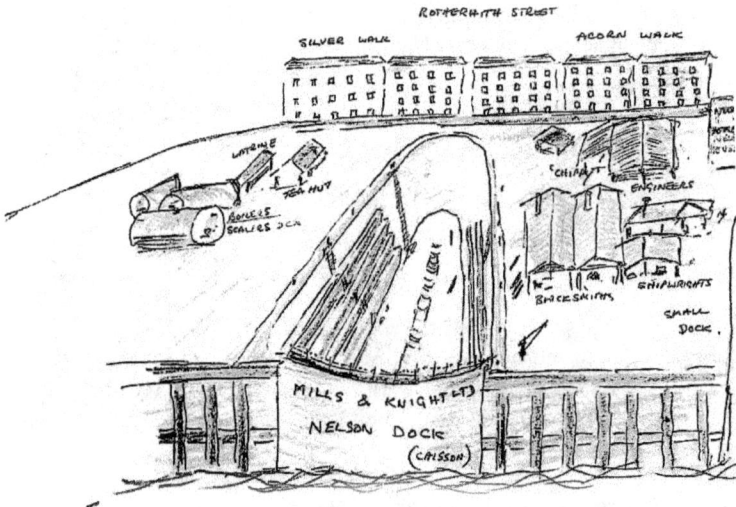

A rough sketch of Nelson dock from the river (1951)

After leaving Mills and Knight and only 11 months at Queen Mary's hospital
I received this. Quite a shock!

Basic training squad in best BD. I am bottom row 3rd right.

Same squad after passing out parade. Relaxing!!
I am back row 1st right (note white washed stones etc)

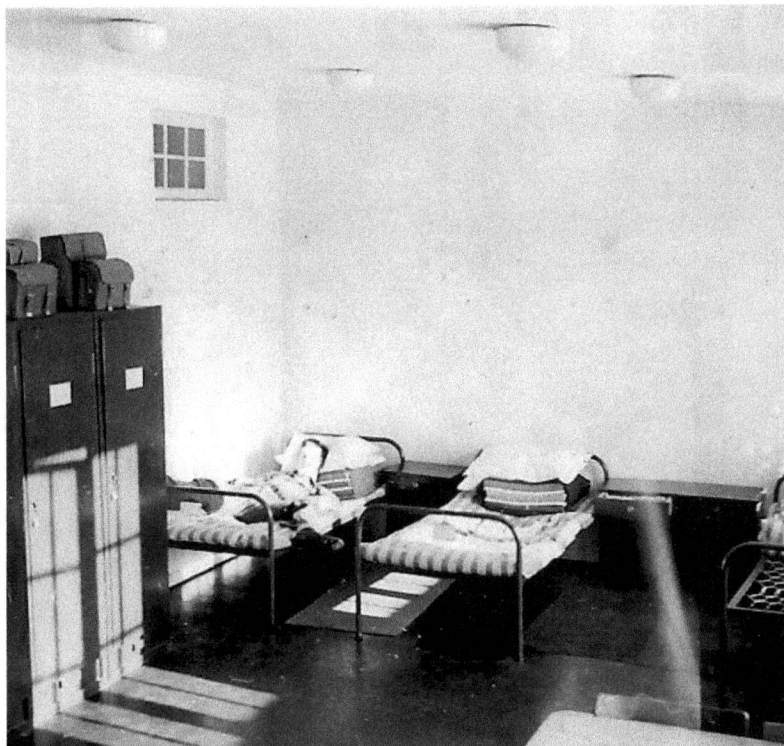

Barrack room after Wednesday morning inspection. George is having a lie in

'Battle Royal'. Our capture due to the dog wanting to play

Staff of Central Pathology Department Münster

Münster BMH Early evening I'm ready to go into Münster town
for good food and a drink.

BMH Münster (today the Universitäts Klinique)

Chapter 7

Called up

In January of the New Year I received a bit of a shock in the post. It was an OHMS letter asking me to present myself at the Wanstead recruitment centre to do my National Service. Although I had spoken to Don about his time in the Medical Corps I naively did not consider myself as eligible. Whilst working as a marine engineering apprentice I had been exempt. Now I was not. At the age of eighteen I was to start a new career in March as a medical laboratory technician in the Royal Army Medical Corps. However I was unaware that I did not have absolute choice as to what and where I was to become and to go. I had only been at Queen Mary's Hospital for about seven months.

I was ordered to appear at the centre in the morning. I sat at a table with about fifteen others in what resembled a small classroom, not thinking I had a choice as to whether I wanted to join the Navy or the Royal Air Force. However I was told that there were no vacancies in their medical departments.

We were given little test papers in English Grammar, Mathematics and some general knowledge. They were about the standard of the eleven-plus papers. A few of the recruits could hardly read or write except for an untidy scrawl for their names at the top of the test paper. I helped two of them either side of me but could not do any more for them. At the end of the test we had to put down in order of preference what branch of the service we wanted. I wrote RAMC (1) RAMC (2) and RAMC (3). I was told I could not do this, but I replied I was not interested in anything else as I worked in a hospital, and this was accepted. My intake number was 54-03. This meant I had until March before reporting.

I told the chief technician that I had been called up. He showed no surprise or concern, possibly because Don had just done his two years' National Service. I spent some time with him discussing the RAMC and what he did during his two years. He was fortunate to work in the laboratories as he did in civvy street. This was obviously my aim too, although my short experience in the laboratories was against me and I might end up as a nurse.

When the time came, having read my rail pass and other papers, I travelled with my mother, father and brother to Waterloo Station. I was being sent to the Queen Elizabeth Barracks, Mytchett, Crookham in Hampshire, close to Aldershot. It was Thursday the fourth of March. This was the RAMC basic training centre. The nearest station was Fleet. My mother cried as I waved them goodbye from the carriage window. As the steam train got under way I put my holdall containing sandwiches and a change of underwear up on the luggage rack. The only other person in the carriage was a lad about my age sitting smoking a cigarette watching me. He nodded and offered me a cigarette, which I accepted. He told me he was going to Fleet. This was pleasing as I was beginning to have a strong feeling of loneliness. We were both apprehensive, as neither of us had any idea what was lying ahead.

We arrived at the station. As soon as our feet touched the

platform there was a bellow: 'Right lads this way! Show your passes and jump into the lorries outside.'

There were two lorries to take thirty-plus boys from the train. The lorries, canvas covered with a high tailgate, drove off. Some lads were standing and hanging onto the metal hoops holding up the canvas, others sat around the sides. I was standing. It was a very bumpy and uncomfortable ride. We reached the barracks. 'Right lads, all out. Stand by the road in single file.' He was a corporal, very smart with his brasses on his belt and his buttons shining brightly. His gaiters and his belt were blancoed green. Most noticeable however were his boots. I had never seen anything like it. The toecaps were like mirrors glinting in the sun. His peaked cap was set straight and the peak rested on his nose so that you could hardly see his eyes. We all lined up. He marched towards us, stamping his feet and looking us up and down. No expression on his face, his back and head perfectly straight.

'Right my beauties,' he said. 'You are now in the army and you belong to me.' Someone made a little noise. 'Silence' he shouted.

I began to realise that I had no more freedom. I could not question a point, let alone argue, or I would suffer the consequences. You did exactly what you were told, immediately.

'I will call out your names.' He produced a clipboard. 'You will take a step forward and shout 'Here corporal'. Got it?'

Someone said 'Yes sir'. The corporal glared at the lad. 'Sir? Sir? Do you see any bird shit on my shoulders? What are these on my sleeves laddie?'

'Stripes sir' said the boy.

'They are chevrons denoting my rank as corporal, got it?' shouted the corporal.

'Yes sir' was the reply.

'Not sir, you idiot. What are you?' shouted the corporal.

'An idiot, corporal' replied the lad.

'That's better' said the corporal. There was a little movement of his mouth which I think was a smile. He started the roll call. We all complied correctly and he seemed satisfied.

'Right' said the corporal, 'Pick up your gear and follow me'. We were marched to several long huts that were facing towards a centre point like spokes in a wheel. It was known as the 'spider', presumably because of the resemblance to a spider's web. We entered a barrack room, about twenty of us. It was empty of people. There were several other 'spiders' and administration and medical areas. There were gates at the entrance which we drove through in the lorry, flanked by brick buildings. This was the guardroom or 'glasshouse'. There were also larger wooden buildings. These were the cookhouses, gymnasium and lecture rooms. Close to the cookhouse was a huge concreted square of several acres. This was the drill square, which I would get to know well and loathe. The barrack room that we were herded into had ten iron beds each side interspaced with wooden lockers. There was a small room at the entrance end of the barrack. This was our Squad Corporal's room.

On the wooden floor there was a black line about two inches wide running the length of the barrack at the foot of the beds to enable us to keep our beds in perfect alignment. Someone in the past had this brilliant idea to keep the beds in line, and unfortunately the army took the idea on board and since then the black line had to be applied with boot black and polished every morning. Under each window between the beds hung two fire buckets, one filled with water the other sand. There was no heating in the barrack room.

We placed our gear in the lockers and were then marched in an ungainly fashion to a large wooden building. This was the storeroom. At the door we were stopped and one by one allowed in. A sergeant roughly measured us and sent us further into the building. There was another sergeant behind a very long counter.

Behind him shelf upon shelf of khaki clothes were neatly stacked. A cardboard box was shoved in front of me and in it were placed articles of clothing with accompanying shouts of what the article was by the sergeant, who at the same time was ticking them off on a card. 'Beret one, Badge one, blouse two, drawers cellulose green underwear for the use of two, socks pair two, housewife one, buttons brass polisher for the use of one, belt, gaiters' and so on. Last but not least a copy of the corps book, 'Not least in the Crusade'. This was a short history of the RAMC.

We carried the boxes outside and placed them at our feet. We were also given a burgundy-coloured lanyard to wear around our left shoulder and the end tucked into the left breast pocket and two blue cotton 'flashes' to fix on our shoulder flaps. These were an indication of what squad we belonged to, and they also indicated to everyone that we were 'sprogs', in other words new recruits. We stood there waiting for the rest of the squad. We then marched back to our barrack room. The rest of the afternoon was ours, in so far as we had to spend the time trying on our equipment. Unlike the soldiers I had seen in the camp, my beret was fluffy, my brasses dull, my belt untreated with blanco and my boots were 'bobbly' and not smooth and mirror-like.

Our squad corporal came in. 'Right lads' he shouted, 'Listen up. I am your corporal and everything I say you answer 'Yes corporal'. When I give you an order you will do it immediately and at the double. Now you will all parade outside in three ranks with your uniforms on'.

We dressed as well as we could and paraded outside. The first thing he showed us was the right way to wear the beret. One side had to be pulled down over the right ear and the badge vertically in line with the left eye. Most efforts were nothing like the corporal's and looked very comical. Some resembled a scholar's mortarboard because they would not stay down. However we did not dare laugh. Gaiters were upside down and round the wrong way and some under the trouser bottoms.

He went down the line. Each man had to take a step forward as he faced the corporal. As he adjusted your gear he shouted out what had to be done. For example, 'Move your cap badge to the right position by drawing your index finger – what's your index finger laddie? Yes that one, not the one you pick your nose with. Now draw it down so that it's over your left eyeball.'

Our belt buckles were adjusted, gaiters corrected and buttons all done up. Our ties, unlike the corporal's, were all fluffy. Apparently they got better after boiling. We were now marched off erratically, to the disgust of the corporal, to the barber's to get our hair cut. The barber may have had some qualifications, but I didn't think it mattered. The term 'haircut' was not accurate. 'Shave' was a better term.

I sat down in a chair ankle deep in hair and removed my beret.

'How would you like it sir?' asked the soldier. 'Just a trim?' It mattered not what you said. No scissors were to be seen. The clippers started from the back of my neck and went over to my forehead. My beret, when placed back on my head, was no longer a tight fit. Some of the recruits had styled and longish hair and they were visibly shocked and upset.

We paraded outside and when all were shorn the squad was marched to the next hut. It was a long hut with many tables. Here I was given my 'dog tags'- blank. I was given my army number, 230008809. This I was to remember. It had to be given whenever your name was called and to collect your pay. Usually just the last three digits sufficed, but any serviceman, no matter how old, if asked would reel off his number unhesitatingly. This I have checked even today and not one person has failed. Years later one man in hospital, dying, suddenly sat up in bed and shouted out. I was asked what on earth he said. I replied it was his service number. He fell back dead.

On other tables we found metal stamps and hammers. We had to punch our number, name and religion, for instance C of E or RC, and some stamped out 'Atheist' which was frowned upon but had to be accepted. This chore done, we were marched back to our barrack room and given a demonstration by the corporal on how to polish our boots and iron our blouses, trousers and shirts. I was beginning to find that in the services there was bags of bull. Bull is army for bullshit and means excessive cleaning and plenty of 'swank'. If it moved, salute, it if it didn't then paint it or polish it. Boots were of prime importance. To remove the bobbly surface on the toe cap and heel we smeared boot polish on thickly. A spoon was an important tool for the job. The toecap was set alight. As it burned the spoon was used, pressing down hard and smoothing the polish over the bobbles. This was done several times, toe and heel, until the bobbles were smoothed out. The boot was then polished in the usual army way using a rag and index finger making small circular movements and spitting on the boot often, hence the term 'spit and polish'. This was done every night before getting into bed until they were like mirrors so that the corporal would not have to shout 'I want to see your 'orrible face in them!' It was like a religion. Soldiers would be sitting on their beds chatting away making circular polishing movements. It became the most important thing in the recruits' life.

The following morning we were awakened at five am. Our beds were kicked and whacked with the corporal's swagger stick to his shout of 'Hands off cocks and on socks you lazy bastards. I want you outside in three ranks in thirty minutes'. The attitude of our corporal was now a little different. He was more officious.

The barrack room was chaotic. Everyone was rushing around, dashing to the washrooms for our ablutions, dressing and making our beds and boxing our blankets. That meant a folded blanket, a folded sheet, another folded blanket and again a sheet followed by another blanket. This sandwich was wrapped with another blanket put at the head of the bed and topped with a steel helmet looking like a slice from a Battenberg cake. The bed was made hospital fashion with enveloped corners.

When we got outside the barrack room we lined up in three ranks as best we could.

'Right you 'orrible lot you look a bloody mess. What are you?'

'A bloody mess, corporal' we replied.

'I can't hear you!'

At the top of our voices we shouted 'A bloody mess corporal!'

'Right get back to your barrack room. Wait for it! Wait till I give you the command. Now left wheel by the left quick march. Jesus Christ, forget it. Just get back in the barrack room.' We straggled back in.

'Stand by your beds. Right, your backpack has to be squared and put on top of your locker.' 'Squared' meant that squares of cardboard had to be cut to fit the sides of the pack so that they were rigid and absolutely square. This applied to everything, including socks for inspection when placed on the bed.

Our civilian clothes, 'civvies', were parcelled up and sent home. Once that was done I realised that I was definitely army property and the corporal owned me.

The next morning we were marched off with a great deal of shouting by the corporal to the medical wing to be inoculated for smallpox, tetanus and typhoid A and B. We had to 'Drop 'em soldier' and give the regulation cough whilst the medic cradled our testicles. Then 'Bend over laddie' and the medic with a little torch peered up and around the anal region. There were a few immediate casualties, as some fainted at the sight of the needle. The next day there were a few more as we had to march with stiff sore arms regardless, swinging them breast pocket high. Some had to go to sickbay.

From now on it was marching. Every day we were up at five am and out on parade drill for an hour before breakfast. Our knives, forks and mugs after use had to be cleaned, and this was done on leaving the cookhouse. Outside the cookhouse the steam from the boilers went into an open tank. The water was scalding hot and you had to dip the utensils in and whiz them about. If they were dropped, you could only retrieve them at night when the tank had cooled by reaching down to your armpits to the bottom of the tank. The utensils and mug were not just for eating but had to be laid out for inspection each morning on your bed, so they had to be retrieved that evening.

From now on our training was mainly marching drill. 'Right Marker' meant the soldier on the right took two paces forward smartly. 'Tallest on the left and right, shortest in the middle, squad, dress to the right' meant taking two paces forward and then with our right arms outstretched touching the shoulder of the soldier to your right. Heads turned in the same direction, we shuffled until we were in line with the 'right marker'. This was after the confusion of sorting out who was short and who was tall.

Not that the commands were pronounced as such. 'Teeeeen [pause] SHUN' was attention. 'Byeeeeeeeeee, wait for it' – threateningly – pause – 'queeeek hip – 'eft, 'eft 'eft 'ight 'eft. Squaaaaaaad, pause, halt!' As we did so we shouted out 'One, one two', lifting our legs and stamping our boots down, one followed by the other.

'Stand still!' shouted the corporal. If a soldier was not quick enough, the corporal would then go up to him nose to nose and shout at him.

The most intimidating, I found, was the drill sergeant. He was about five foot six inches tall and his usual address to a soldier was 'You, little man, come here'. He had a peaked cap with the peak bent vertically down so that it practically hid his eyes like a visor. He would shout at you face to face, flecks of saliva striking your face. You did not dare bat an eyelid or look at him as he shouted, 'You, little man. What are you looking at? Look to your front you bloody nignog. What are you?'

'A bloody nignog, sergeant' was the replied shout.

'Can't hear you.'

'A bloody nignog, sergeant.'

The sergeant marched everywhere and appeared to have a board up his back and a large swagger stick, which was in fact a wooden calliper to measure our marching stride. After we'd had a few weeks of this we carried out all commands instantaneously to the satisfaction of our squad corporal. We were however marched to the parade ground to have our drill a little more refined by a drill sergeant on loan from one of the Guards Regiments.

We stood at ease. A tall soldier immaculately dressed and straight as a board with a shiny black peak straight down over his nose, he marched on to the parade ground a hundred yards or so from us. His trouser creases were as sharp and straight as knives. His boots and belt brasses were dazzling. The stick under his arm was similar to our drill sergeant's stick. His demeanour put the fear of God into us immediately. I say 'us' because there was slight shuffling and swallowing either side of me. Even our corporal seemed anxious. These feelings were accentuated when he bellowed from about one hundred feet, 'That man, second from the right, straighten your left gaiter and do your top button up'. The soldier took a step forward, adjusted his gaiter and did up his button. It was only half way in the eye of the buttonhole. The sergeant must have had the eye of an eagle. I was amazed.

At attention our feet had to be heels together with the toe of the boots at an angle of approximately forty-five degrees. A soldier with his toecaps too close together would have the drill sergeant's boot slamming them apart until they were at the right angle.

I found the most difficult part was marching in three ranks and then the order to left turn and march line abreast ready for the eyes right or left command. It usually ended up at first with the middle or back rank colliding with the rank in front when the eyes right command was given. This caused the drill sergeant to scream at us in no uncertain terms.

There were unfortunately some soldiers who found it difficult to march. They walked in the normal manner with the right foot forward and left arm swinging forward, but when it came to marching it all went wrong, with the right foot forward and right arm swung forward at the same time. The swaggering penguin gait was quite comical, but no one dared to laugh. It took our corporal a whole week to get them straightened out and marching properly. One or two could not ascertain which foot was right and which was left and had to have a piece of straw tucked in their bootlace. So for them it was 'by the straw foot quick march'.

Although the RAMC was a non–combatant unit, we were still required to familiarise ourselves with various weapons, especially the Lee Enfield 303 rifle. There were Bren and Sten guns and Mills hand grenades, but the weapon we had to use was the 303.

On the rifle range I had no problems. Just after the war I belonged to the Barking Power Station rifle club using a BSA Martini .22, but after an eye test in the army I was told I was myopic and had to go to Colchester to the Royal Army Medical Corp Military hospital to get army regulation wire-rimmed spectacles. Before I could get good groupings on the target on the range, but as soon as I put the glasses on, although I could see much more clearly, the target looked smaller and I missed the bull. The Lee Enfield had a five-round clip and on one occasion I could not hit the bull, so I removed my specs.

'What ter blooty hell's wrong wit yow?' shouted our instructor, who was from the Irish Fusiliers. 'Keep yer glasses on!' I lay down in the prone position again and fired my last two rounds. The results could not be seen on my target. I assumed that they had gone through the holes of my previous rounds. However it was found that the soldier to my left had seven rounds on his target, so two of them must have been mine. Previously I had seen a large, blurred bull and centred on this with success. I began to realise what I had been missing all my life. I could see things in a different light. I did not have to wear them all the time, only at classes and on the firing range. If you wore them with your steel helmet, not the First World War and Second World War version but similar to the American style, they got in the way of the chinstrap and kept moving up and down. I remember at school I passed a sight test by memorising what the boy in front had called out when looking at the letters.

Our important piece of equipment was our water bottle, which had to be kept in pristine condition, especially on the inside, and was not for our personal use!

Drill, rifle practice, assault courses and lectures on syphilis and gonorrhoea, nursing procedures, field ambulance training and first aid were the weekly norm. Once a week we had to put up large tents and huge marquees in fifteen minutes flat. This was achievable when it was not windy, but at a demonstration watched by one of our officers on a windy day we had difficulty. We could not pull the marquee upright using the guy ropes, even with ten soldiers pulling hard. The corporal was running around shouting orders. He was unfortunately on the other side of the marquee with the sergeant. The marquee was to be a field operating theatre. The officer was standing well back.

A gust of wind was too much for us and pulled the ropes out of some of the soldiers' hands, so the rest were being dragged along by the marquee, which was now a huge sail. It collapsed away from us but on top of the corporal and the sergeant. We scrambled around to the other side and hauled the heavy canvas off the NCOs (non-commissioned officers). The only damage done was to their pride, except that the sergeant's peaked cap had half the peak broken off. We were all put on defaulters parade at 6 pm after our evening meal. We were paraded outside the Admin Block in our fatigues, belt, boots, gaiters and berets. We had to run at the double around the camp for an hour with stops for a couple of press- ups. After being dismissed we had all our bulling to catch up on, including the barrack room for inspection and all our kit to be laid out on our beds in their proper positions for officer's inspection.

Fatigues/denims were worn for general duties during the day. Our BD (battledress) was for parades etc and a spare including spare boots for show, really, as they were kept pristine for inspection on our beds. The spare boots were usually immaculate with the underside polished black too and all the studs shiny and complete in number.

Monday was laundry day and dirty clothes had to be bagged up neatly and square with a note listing the contents and finishing with name rank and, the last three numbers of your army number, and finally with 'Your obedient servant'.

The 'housewives' issued to us became very useful as our socks soon developed holes which we had to darn. Some soldiers however took shortcuts and did not darn but squeezed the hole together and stitched it closed, making a horrible knot. This was not very comfortable for marching. Some did not bother and used the holed socks for inspection folded so that the tops only showed. If an officer looked carefully and undid the fold the rest of the sock looking like a lace doily would be exposed and he would be for the guardhouse. Again if your brass button polisher guard was not used properly you would end up with a black smudge around your buttons from the Brasso, and once again those guilty would either end up for a spell in the guardhouse or on defaulters' parade.

Some of our basic training was going over the assault courses. Up the ropes we went and over the brick walls, swinging like

Tarzan over deep, muddy ditches and crossing streams on two ropes, and sometimes bayonet practice with a stuffed bag as the enemy, which was a puzzle as we were a non–combatant unit.

Halfway through our basic training we started our medical training. This consisted of nursing procedures including first aid lectures. Most enjoyable for me were the manoeuvres out in the fields surrounding the camp.

We were driven in trucks to the outskirts of Mytchett and dropped off. We unloaded from another lorry stretchers and blankets. It was raining, not very heavily but the ground was wet and muddy. Looking around we could see a few trees in the distance with many ditches and hillocks and a stream about three feet wide. The lorries drove off after we were instructed as to our objective, which was to spread out with stretchers in teams of four or five. The fifth soldier sometimes carried a rifle, which we had to use as a splint if necessary. We had to advance over the ground to look for casualties, as it was supposed to be during a battle and it was made a little realistic by bangers going off and Bren gun fire with smoke bombs being thrown by someone we could not see. There were four teams in all. Some squads had been sent ahead to act as 'casualties' with a label tied to them indicating their injury, bullet in the chest, broken leg, burns etc. We had to find them.

A unit of the RAMC were known as the casualty unit and were expert make-up artists. The wounded looked very realistic, with gunshot wounds to the chest bleeding and frothing when the soldier breathed, activated by a hidden rubber bulb and tube squeezed at the right time, and broken limbs with bones sticking through battledress trousers and burns showing skin peeling away. They were true artists, and this made some soldiers feel a bit queasy.

I was number one in our team of four. We picked up our stretcher containing three blankets and attached our belt and shoulder webbing to the stretcher poles that were threaded through the canvas of the stretcher, then we set off towards the copse about a quarter of a mile away. We stepped off together inside leg first, but if it was only two on the stretcher then you started off out of step to keep the stretcher on even keel.

After only a short distance it became more of a shuffle.

Trotting towards the copse, we crossed the stream and a couple of ditches but could not see any casualties. After searching around, number three of our team heard something in the trees. Looking up we could see a soldier about ten feet up straddled across two of the lower branches.

'What the bloody hell are you doing up there?' said number two. 'Come on down.'

'No mate' said the casualty, 'my label says I've bin blown up by a shell and both my legs are broken.'

'We're not bloody well climbing up that tree,' replied number two.

'You are,' said the casualty.

We all looked at each other. Number three picked up a clod of earth and grass. We were all in accord and started pelting the 'casualty'.

'Bloody well come down or we'll knock you down', number two shouted.

'For fuck sake OK' he said and grabbing a branch, he swung down to the ground.

'Right Jack' I said, 'Let's have a look at your label'. He was right. The label stated two broken legs.

'It doesn't say anything about being blown up a tree' I shouted at him. 'Get him onto the stretcher.'

'We need to put a splint on him,' said number three.

'Get a branch or two from the trees. It's only for show anyway,' I said.

Number three climbed up the tree and broke off two branches.

We stuffed one between his legs and the other on the outside of his leg. We secured them with his denim jacket sleeves, tied around the branches and knotted. We then wrapped him in blankets folded as taught in such a way that he could not move. With leather straps we buckled him to the stretcher. The stretcher poles had metal 'U' shaped legs so that at rest the canvas was just clear of the ground.

We lifted him with a grunt. He was somewhat 'tubby'. Then we started back to base accompanied by what sounded like firecrackers and rifle fire a little way off to give a little authenticity.

As we reached one of the ditches there was a loud shout from a hailer: 'Take cover!' At this command we had to drop flat. We did. The casualty went down heavily with a grunt. I think he was comfortable and had been dozing at the time. A whistle sounded, meaning we were to proceed.

A minute later again 'Take cover!' Unfortunately we were manoeuvring the stretcher across the stream. We dropped down flat with the stretcher half way up the bank. It rolled, and in the stream went our casualty.

'What are you fucking playing at?' shouted the wet casualty.

'Shut up and keep still' said number four with menace. We were supposed to show compassion to a casualty, but a casualty trying to be clever climbing up a tree did not go down well. He was almost face down in the mud under the stretcher. When the whistle blew we pulled him upright with difficulty, as the wet blankets made the stretcher heavy. To make matters worse one of the stewards, who we could not see, shouted, 'Number four, you've been hit, move out.' We could hear other shouts and other stretcher-bearers being 'shot' or hit by imaginary shrapnel.

That left three in our party, two in front and one behind holding both poles, the foot end not being so heavy. We struggled on. About a hundred yards from base we 'took cover' another three times and I lost the rest of my men. The whistle blew. I attached my shoulder webbing to my belt and one of the 'U' shaped legs and half crouching proceeded to drag the stretcher the rest of the way. The legs dragged in the mud but I made slow progress. I was glad when another 'Take cover' was called.

After the whistle there was no more. I got to the base, where there were many other stretchers and casualties. A sergeant looked me up and down and examined the casualty and the blankets, which he unwrapped. He looked at me quickly, smiled and said 'Well done' and moved off. All I could think about was getting all my equipment cleaned when we got back to barracks. My fatigues were covered in mud.

During one of the sessions in the gymnasium we were told to climb ropes and do press-ups and general exercises by a physical training instructor who was short with bulging biceps and it seemed no neck, a thin black moustache and a barrel chest. We were called together and told that there was a boxing competition against other units. 'Are there any boxers here?' he asked. There were some, but obviously not enough. Soldiers who looked the part were 'volunteered' for training. I crouched low and was passed by, but was afterwards picked for the wrestling team. I was about eleven and a half stone in weight at the time. We had been instructed in the art of unarmed combat commando style, which was somewhat far removed from the Queensberry rules. We were not allowed to use this knowledge during our bouts.

One morning we were awakened in the usual manner with accompanying pleasantries, but our squad corporal went berserk. I hadn't noticed, but two soldiers who slept near the doorway were missing. They had deserted during the night or early morning. After finishing our ablutions and breakfast we were stood to attention with the usual order 'Stand by your beds', as if for an inspection. The corporal, two sergeants and an officer questioned us, especially the two soldiers who slept opposite the deserters. We had a lecture afterwards from our corporal, who told us that when they were caught they would get two years in the 'glasshouse' (jail) and when they were released they would still have to complete their National Service, four years altogether. Was it worth it? I could not imagine having two years of hardship and then have to go through another two years. They were caught two weeks later by the Military Police, known as Redcaps, in Fishguard on their way to cross the sea to Ireland.

During this early period of our training there were two suicides, not in our squad but from two others. They were found hanging from their webbing and bootlaces.

Some soldiers were not very good with their hygiene and if dirt and smell were detected on a soldier by our corporal then we were ordered to strip him in the ablutions and scrub him with a floor scrubbing brush, very painful, but it usually did the trick. We were told in future to deal with the problem ourselves for our own health.

During my first couple of months out of the three required for basic training it was very cold. I started on the fourth of March 1954. My intake number was 54:03.

Fire buckets that contained water were frozen, and they had to be replaced with fresh water before inspection. When marching along the icy roads to the parade ground we were often given the order to 'shorten step' to stop us slipping over. However shortening the step often resulted in men falling on their backsides and bringing the rest of the squad with them, much to the disgust of our corporal.

In April we had a 'General Officer Commanding' (GOC) inspection. This incorporated the RAMC band playing 'A Health Unto Her Majesty', the corps march composed by Major Thornburrow, Director of Music of The Royal Horse Guards. So an intensive regime of parades, inspection and drills ensued before the actual GOC parade. National Service Officers were also required on parade. This was the only time we saw them. They were medically qualified.

We were told to wipe the smiles off our faces. We were smiling because of the officers' dress, gaiters undone, belts hanging loosely and peaked caps at all angles. The RSM (Regimental Sergeant Major) was shouting at them and addressing them as 'Mister'. They would not be addressed as 'Sir' until they had finished their basic training. They however, like us, addressed the RSM as 'Sir'.

One of the lads from another squad mumbled something and began to giggle. He was immediately marched off double time between two lance corporals to the guardroom.

We were inspected with the usual 'Am I hurting you laddie?' 'No corporal.' 'Well I should be, I'm bloody well standing on your hair. Get it cut!' And 'Get your trousers sorted in your gaiters'. To keep the trousers hanging neatly in and over the gaiter tops, lead weights or pennies were used to weigh them down evenly. To get fine straight creases in the trousers and in the blouse pleats you would turn the trousers inside out, carefully shave the crease with a razor blade and then turn the trousers back again and iron the creases. However if overdone, the trouser would split down the crease. This I have seen. The guilty soldier would be put on fatigue duty and would also have to pay for a new pair. Those that burnt their boots through to the canvas when trying to remove the bobbles had the same punishment. The corps badge was polished to a high degree, but no polish was allowed to linger in the crevices and in the motto, which was 'In Arduis Fidelis' (faithful in adversity).

We were put through our paces. Marching in ranks of three was fine, but a left turn so that we were three abreast and to execute the salute of 'Eyes right' was not easy. At the given command of 'I-eeeeeeees right!' you snapped your head to your right shoulder, but at the same time you had to watch the rank in front and the soldiers to your right and left as this would often result in collisions, causing apoplexy with our squad corporals.

When the day arrived for our GOC's inspection and parade,

the bulling was way over the top. Grass cut, stones whitewashed, kit laid out on beds millimetre perfect. The joke around the camp was that if it moves salute it, if it doesn't, paint it. This was not far from the truth.

Our marching had to be carried out, as the sergeants ordered us, with 'bags of swank'. They insisted that our swinging arms came up to breast pocket height.

'What do you think you are laddie, a fucking sow with twenty tits down the belly?' was the usual shout from our corporal.

We were marched around the whole of the Elizabeth Barracks. It started to rain, but we were not allowed our rain capes and it was cold but no greatcoats.

We marched on, came to a halt and then it was 'Right marker, right dress, tallest to the left and right, shortest in the middle' and then ordered to stand to attention for five minutes and then stand at ease for ten minutes, then stand easy for another ten minutes so that we could relax. This went on for almost an hour before the adjutant standing in for the GOC took the salute. This was just practice for the passing out parade when the GOC would take the salute. Any soldier who fainted was charged, as it was assumed he had not had breakfast. To help when standing at ease, we stretched up on our toes.

In between all this we had to train for our Nursing Orderly Class III exams and then to do our bulling for the usual morning inspections. During this period the soldiers in the squad became very close and began to understand the meaning of comradeship and also to learn other people's way of life and to understand their various dialects, because there were Scots, Irish, Welsh and dialects from every county. Some were very difficult to understand at first especially the 'Geordies'. It was a good education for me in that respect.

Wednesdays were sports afternoons and I went in for cross-country running. When training for this we wore vests, shorts, socks and boots with a backpack containing a couple of bricks. Running wearing army boots and long black shorts looked very odd. We carried the bricks when only two miles were to be run. For a five-mile run we discarded the pack altogether.

During one cross-country race I found myself in fifth place. Ahead in the lead were the corps champions, two lads who were twins. I thought I might be able to catch up as I was feeling fine. We were three quarters into the race and instead of running through the five-barred gate leading onto the road back to camp I decided to leap the hedge onto the road, taking a legal short cut. As I cleared the hedge, both legs tucked, my calf muscles went.

Cramp or torn muscles? I was not sure, but I collapsed onto the road, crashing into a ditch. I had to be half-dragged and half-carried back to camp by a corporal whilst another rubbed my calves and applied wet cold leaves, which made no difference. If I had not leapt the hedge I think I would have stood a chance of at least coming third.

Towards the end of my basic training I was summoned by the Commanding Officer, a colonel. I marched into his office, stamped to attention, saluted and gave my name and last three numbers. He asked me, after telling me to stand at ease and then to stand easy, what branch of the RAMC I would like to work in. 'Pathology' I replied, because I was doing that before being called up. 'Well,' said the colonel, 'There may be a position, but that is not a certainty. What other branch would you be prepared to go in if there are no vacancies? There's STN, that's Special Treatment Nursing involving syphilis etc, psychiatric nursing or there's the Paramedics.' I said I had not considered anything else but pathology, but if necessary I would opt for Paramedics.

'Very well my boy, we shall see' said the colonel and dismissed me. I gave a half-hearted salute, about turned and left the room. I was worried about where I would end up and my stomach pained me. I suffered on occasion with nervous dyspepsia which was started off by such problems.

When the end of my basic training was three weeks away there was still no word and the drill sergeant and my corporal told me I was to go for paramedic training. I was not very pleased. I had to do more first aid training and was sent to Blackbushe near Aldershot with the Parachute Regiment with eight others. We did a lot of running, which was OK, but shovelling coal from one side of the road to the other and then being told to shovel it back again was back-breaking work. I enjoyed their assault courses however. We had to learn how to fall with legs together and roll to one side.

There were pylons where one is suspended and let down as if attached to a parachute. This was a bit hair-raising as it was pretty high. The following Thursday I was to go up in a sort of small topless railway carriage attached to a barrage balloon and jump with chute and the following Thursday a proper jump from a Dakota. I was not looking forward to it at all.

However, to my relief I was called back to barracks, where I was told by the RSM that I had a posting to the Royal Army Medical College at Millbank, London, and with the other lab tech in our squad, who was from Somerset, I was to report in two weeks' time. I was over the moon. The most pleasing part was that we would miss the passing-out parade and GOC's inspection. Also six other 'sprogs', as we new intakes were called, were also posted to various units.

For the first time during our stay at training camp, we were all allowed an evening pass into Aldershot. Before we could go however, we had to get past the gate inspection. If we were not one hundred percent immaculate we would be sent back to get the offending problem righted, ie a bit of blanco found in a belt eyelet would be sufficient cause. Some never made it outside the barracks – they gave up after being sent back too many times.

With three others, I made it after a couple of attempts. We bussed into Aldershot and had some beers in the various pubs. Most were full of soldiers and comments made towards us 'sprogs' (denoted by our shoulder flashes) were ignored. There were fights however at closing time and Military Police seemed to be busy. We had to run to catch the last bus back to barracks. Here again we were inspected and sent on our way.

Before our departure date came we were sent on guard duty one night to the transport compound. It was cold, so we wore our greatcoats. It was a concreted area with a metal gate that had a pillbox where we had to stand. We had two hours on and four hours off duty as our rota. In a small hut there were a couple of bunks, uncomfortable and not conducive to a decent sleep. Our greatcoats were heavy and uncomfortable, but they were warm. During our stint two lorries came and were signed in. It was very boring. Our squad corporal tried to relieve this boredom. He attempted to test us by creeping up to us and catching us unawares.

We heard a noise in the bushes across the road from the gate. 'What's that?' said one of the team. 'Probably a fox' I said. We stayed quiet, all four of us. No one was asleep. We listened. There was another movement from another bush. 'That's not a fox. I've heard that the squad corporals try to catch the guards off guard,' whispered one of the team. He reached inside the pillbox and picked up a chair leg, which seemed our only means of defence if there was an enemy attack. He walked out past the gate and ran straight at the bushes opposite. When he reached the first bush he swung the chair leg down onto the bush with a crash. Nothing moved, but a shout from the bush close to it startled us. Our squad corporal stood up and then a lance corporal from another bush stood up. 'All right lads, that will do' he said. 'Get back to your posts.' He was a little upset that he had been spotted in the dark, so he lined us up and inspected us, bawling out one of the lads for having the top button of his greatcoat undone. The next time we saw him was when he marched in our relief squad at three am and then marched us off back to our barrack room.

We were told regularly that at any command we were to drop everything and go when required. During fire picket duty we were sitting drinking cocoa in the cookhouse when the fire whistle went. We jumped up, throwing our cocoa in the sinks where some soldiers on fatigue duty were washing up and covering some of them in hot cocoa. Out we went onto the road outside at the double. The sergeant in charge of fire picket duties was waiting for us already. We ran in step to where the fire was supposed to be. It could be the real thing or just another practice. At either side of the pathways as one got to the barrack rooms there were two concrete posts about three feet high with one in the middle of the path. The reason for their existence I never questioned. I think they were there just to be painted white. However the first six of us passed through at the run, but the last two did not see the centre post and crashed into it. The sergeant ran back after hearing a scream. The lad who had run into the post had broken his leg. He also broke his arm when the other lad fell on top of him, and here I witnessed the efficiency of our training. The sergeant strapped his legs and arm using his belt and swagger stick as a splint and sent two lads off to get a stretcher and inform the sick bay. We also used our belts, but it was the sergeant, feeling the screaming soldier's leg, who diagnosed the break. After removing his blouse he realised the arm was not fractured but dislocated. He spoke to the lad very quietly and kindly. This was the first sign of compassion from an NCO I had observed since being drafted.

Meal times were always rushed. No time for relaxation. Once the meal was over we had a quick fag, dashed back to the barrack room and changed ready for parade or drill etc.

The two weeks soon passed. For some reason I was given two

chevrons to pin to my arm as a full corporal to take charge of the rail passes and other warrants needed to move out of the barracks. There were six other 'squaddies' for posting to various units in the country. We were all pleased, because we would definitely miss the passing-out parade.

The chevrons made my day complete because the lance corporal involved with our drill and parades (not out squad corporal) was disliked by everyone because of his verbal bullying and keenness to dish out punishments, was pushing his way as usual to the front of the meal queue. This was the Wednesday before we were due to leave. He started shouting to those in the front of the queue to stand aside, his usual ploy, and pushed two soldiers and me out of the way. I went up to him and tapped him on the shoulder. He turned, glared at me and said 'What do you want soldier?' I replied quietly 'Get back to the end of the queue corporal and wait your turn.'

'Do you want to be put on a charge, laddie?' he shouted at me.

'No corporal' I said, 'But if you don't want to be on a charge I suggest you do not disobey my order.' I pointed to the two stripes pinned onto my arm only two hours before. The lance corporal with his one stripe blanched and with mouth open gave a grunt and went back to the end of the queue. Unfortunately he would probably take it out on the other poor squaddies, as with most bullies. Some would say he was only doing his job, but he seemed to enjoy intimidating people far too much. However the others and I were very chuffed.

I collected all the travel warrants and other documents from the office in the admin block at 5 am Thursday morning and signed for them. We were then paraded outside our barrack blocks with all our gear and inspected. The tabs on our shoulder straps were removed, so we were no longer labelled as 'sprogs'.

The lorry to take us to the station was waiting, but the

sergeant took his time inspecting us. He could probably see we were anxious to get out of the training camp. He marched us off to the covered lorry our kit bags atop our backpacks, shouting comments about our kit. The kit bags made marching very awkward, so it was quite a relief to dump them in the back of the lorry. Soon we were off and I noticed everyone was smiling. The journey to the station and the train to London were uneventful, with lots of chatting laughing and smoking. We had no idea what was in store for us, but we were glad to be embarking on this new adventure.

Chapter 8

Royal Army
Medical College

At the station in London I distributed the documents and said cheerio to all except to the other lab tech, Hugh, who had been posted to HQ No. 18 Company Millbank with me. We both grabbed our gear and made our way along the platform, noticing that there were many MPs (Redcaps or Military Police) so we made sure our buttons were done up. A Redcap sergeant asked for our destination and warrants. We gave them to him. He looked us up and down, said 'On your way soldier' and marched away. We got on a tube train to Westminster and walked to Millbank RAM College.

On arrival, sweating and puffing after our walk from the station with all our gear, we walked through the gates to the guardroom reception. We dumped our gear and marched to the desk, where the duty sergeant was writing in a ledger. We came to attention, stamping our feet as trained. This made the sergeant look up. He had a quizzical expression on his face. He smiled. 'Stand easy corporal,' he said to me, 'we don't like too much noise here and you can dispense with all the bullshit. Just salute the officers and keep yourselves tidy and do as you're told. Got it?'

'Yes sergeant' I said, coming to attention. 'No my boy, stand easy and relax' he said quietly.

I handed over our documents and unpinned my stripes. He got on the phone and shortly a staff sergeant came down from the pathological laboratories to meet us. I looked at Hugh and we both smiled. This place seemed very relaxed. What a relief. I had envisaged two more years of training camp attitudes.

The staff sergeant introduced himself. 'I'm Staff Sergeant Yeats and you call me Staff. I'll show you where you're going to live.' It was a Nissen hut with an iron stove and chimney in the middle of the right-hand wall and seemed quite comfortable. The beds were 'made up' with blankets boxed but not neatly, nor were the packs on top of the lockers boxed very well like our training camp.

We stowed our gear and followed him across a parade ground surrounded by old Victorian brick buildings. 'This is the hospital,' he said. We entered one of the buildings and went up a flight of stone stairs. A couple of floors up we reached the pathological departments. The only stairs we had climbed for three months were in the form of ramps and ropes across streams on the assault courses.

Staff Sergeant Yeats entered a door and knocked, then saluted and beckoned us in. We saw a colonel at his desk. We slammed to attention and saluted. He smiled and said quietly 'Relax'. He asked us several questions regarding our previous laboratory experience and whether we had any specialisation in haematology, biochemistry, bacteriology, virology or histology. We both said that we were just student technicians. 'Good' he said. 'We can train you our way, which is the best. We are known throughout the world for our expertise in parasitology and tropical medicine. All overseas service personnel who have become a victim of some disease or another are sent back to the UK here. Staff will be your tutor and in three months you will take your Lab III exam. Any questions?'

'Yes sir' said Hugh, 'If we pass do we stay on here?'

'No,' replied the colonel. 'When you have qualified to our satisfaction there will be vacancies either in this country or overseas. If you're lucky you will get a posting abroad wherever our forces are stationed. If you do not pass however, I'm afraid you will be attached to other units in special treatment centres, psychiatric nursing or just on the wards as a nurse. Maybe if there is a vacancy you could work in a laboratory in the wash -up departments.'

These thoughts gave us a great resolve to succeed.

'All right?' asked the colonel.

'Yes sir' we replied. 'OK staff sergeant, get them started.'

We got started straight away. We were introduced to the rest of the staff. They were obviously posted to Millbank for the rest of their service.

The training for the Lab. III examination was intensive and thorough. The Staff Sergeant gave us work in all the laboratory disciplines throughout our stay.

Every morning there was a parade. Unlike during our basic training the inspection by the RSM (Regimental Sergeant Major) was only rudimentary. You had to look tidy and clean, and that was about it. The roll call, however, was a little bizarre. Some soldiers, those from London who lived at home, came to work by public transport. If they were late for parade it was usually noticed early by someone who worked with him, so one of the soldiers on parade was told to call out 'Sir' when the absentee's name was called. If the soldier appeared however without his alias knowing, there was a duet of 'Sir' which seemed to go unnoticed by the RSM, except for a slight grin on his face. I'm sure he knew.

The lab bench work was busy and the lecture notes prodigious. We were questioned every day until we knew the subject by heart. We participated in post mortem examinations and took scrapings, blood and other body fluids from soldiers who had been abroad, especially in the Far East and Africa, and had been sent home to 'Blighty' (taken from an Urdu word, 'bilayati' bastardised by British soldiers in the Indian army which meant foreign or European. To a British soldier it meant Great Britain).

A high-ranking officer well-known during World War Two, Air Marshall Lord T, came to Millbank for a urine test. The urine was in a conical glass and was tested OK, but when a lance corporal came back to the laboratory after lunch one of the staff said 'I haven't had time to do the test yet' and pointed to the form beneath the glass. The corporal picked up the form and read the name and said sternly 'You should have done this right away'. Unknown to the corporal, the soldier, in league with others, had poured diluted orange juice into another glass and placed it on the form. Testing the urine with Benedict's solution for sugar, the colour turned black in the test tube, showing an extremely positive result. 'Bloody hell,' said the corporal, 'This is ridiculous. It's about twenty percent glucose in this urine.'

'Twenty percent?' said the soldier, 'You must be joking.'

'No' said the corporal. 'Look at the test.'

'Hmmm' said the soldier and dipped his finger in the 'urine' and tasted it. 'About fifteen per cent I'd say.'

The corporal looked at him in astonishment but was even more shocked when one of the other soldiers said 'Fifteen per cent glucose? Lovely', then picked up the glass, sipped it and then drank the whole lot. The corporal's mouth dropped open, but he realised he'd been had when the rest of us began to laugh. 'You silly sods' he said and got on with his work chuckling.

Our Staff Sergeant's lectures were thorough. I remember him telling us about pH and body fluids. He said that semen was alkaline and vaginal secretions were acidic, so that on ejaculation the pH would be neutral for the sperms to travel on their merry way. One bright spark said 'Oh, then my girl can't say 'Don't come the old acid with me then' can she?' The Staff Sergeant thought it funny and used it as his own joke on other trainees.

We were also taken on the wards to take blood and skin scrapes. On one occasion the colonel took us to a soldier's bedside. The soldier had spent years in the Far East. The colonel gently trailed cotton wool along his limbs with the soldier's eyes closed, asking him to say when he could feel the wool. He also took nasal specimens with cotton wool swabs and scrapes with a scalpel. The soldier had leprosy, so he felt no sensation. This we confirmed in the laboratory.

The Queen's birthday was a special occasion at Millbank. We had to be on parade with 100 per cent bull. We had to line The Mall behind the guards in their bearskins waiting for the Queen in her coach to pass. The guards had been standing along the route for hours. Our job was to keep an eye on them in case one of them fainted. I saw two faint. Soldiers fainted by numbers, that is, number one, push aside bayoneted rifle, number two fall to your knees and three complete the faint, at which point the guard was probably not conscious. At this juncture we rushed to the unfortunate guard with water bottle at the ready undoing his high collar removing bearskin and helping him away. This was during Regimental Sergeant Major Britten's career. One could hear his voice of command from one end of The Mall to the other.

After the Queen had passed and I had finished my salute I noticed RSM Britten bollocking the soldier behind the lines, warning him that he would be 'put on a charge for not having your breakfast, laddie'. A stickler for discipline was the RSM.

If an officer was on the telephone to him it was alleged that he would say, 'I am now saluting you sir'. That's the army for you.

All disciplines of pathology were in two large laboratories. The microbiology benches were close to the colonel's and captain's office. The haematology bench was behind the office and the biochemistry, histology and parasitology benches were in a separate room.

Millbank Royal Army Medical College had a superb library and also a museum containing books and microscope slides of every disease, the majority pertaining to the tropics.

A soldier joined a week after us who was a qualified biochemist and was to be made an officer after he took his Lab III exams. Without degrees we would be lucky to make corporal.

Another soldier was employed in the wash-up and sterilisation department. He was a qualified bacteriologist, but because of a motor bike accident he had missed his training and therefore as he only had two months of his National Service to do he was stuck washing and sterilising glassware. This in a way typified the army. He was far more qualified in bacteriology than most of the laboratory staff, but because he had not taken his Lab III examination he was not allowed in the main laboratory. The qualified biochemist who had a BSc degree, after passing his Lab III examination, was asked to stay on at Millbank, become an officer and teach biochemistry.

We all eventually passed our examinations, helped by strict tuition from our Staff Sergeant. He taught us well, but on parade he was about the scruffiest soldier I have seen. His belt could not encompass his waist and was buckled up below the belly. His trouser bottoms were never completely tucked into his gaiters, but he seemed quite unconcerned.

The other regular staff also contributed to our success. They were literally always behind us during the tests making sure we were on the right track. I had an affinity for parasitology and tropical medicine and was impressed with the specimens available for study. I gained full marks in these subjects. Microbiology, biochemistry and haematology subjects I managed quite well, but with histology, the laboratory section of morbid anatomy, eg post-mortems and preparing tissue for microscopic examination looking for abnormal cells and virology, I was not as happy.

The practical part of our examination went smoothly. It consisted of testing for sugar in urines, examining slides under the microscope for malaria and identifying various bacteria and serologically typing in the identification of a salmonella species. In haematology we had to find the blood groups of various blood specimens and cross-match them with other blood specimens to ascertain compatibility as if for blood transfusion.

The oral part of the exams however was quite daunting, as we had to sit in front of our colonel with one major and two captains.

I was asked about the principles and workings of a refrigerator. I was stumped. I had never considered that I might be asked such a question, although part of our work was the maintenance of centrifuges, incubators and fridges, as I had concentrated on other disciplines, especially the life cycles of various parasites.

Fortunately the captain asking the question had a phone call and had to leave. The colonel did not continue on this track and asked me to my relief to tell him the life cycle of the common liver fluke, Fasciola hepatica, which I knew. When the captain returned he was not given the chance to continue with his fridge questions. I breathed a sigh of relief. I did not want to fail after three months' intensive study, coaching and bench work. Happily I passed.

The staff sergeant usually prepared the bodies of soldiers that had died for post mortem examination performed by the colonel, our pathologist. One old soldier who had died of cancer of the bowel was one of the first I attended. We wore masks. This was unusual then and those that smoked were told to light up. The reason for this we soon found out. The soldier's abdomen was extremely distended and the soldier was very large anyway. We had great difficulty getting him off the ambulance into the mortuary.

The Staff Sergeant asked if we were ready. He then inserted a needle into the distended abdomen. The release of gas was enormous. Masks and cigarette smoke helped because the smell was indeed foul. I was a little concerned that our cigarettes might ignite the released methane, but the Staff Sergeant was not concerned.

Chapter 9

The toss of a coin

Two weeks after passing our exam, Hugh and I were asked to report to the colonel at 9 am the following morning. The 'biochemist' was not summoned. We were marched into the colonel's office and told to stand at ease.

'Well lads' said the colonel, 'You are both being posted. The problem is one is to go to Germany and one to Hong Kong. Have either of you a preference?' This was unusual. Normally you did not have a choice – you were told where to go.

We both answered in unison. 'Hong Kong Sir.'

'Oh dear' said the colonel. 'OK Staff, toss a coin.'

'Right you two' said Staff, 'you call, Eldridge.'

'Heads' I called as the coin spun in the air. Staff caught it and showed it to us. It was tails. 'Right lad sort out your gear' he said to Hugh, 'You're off to Hong Kong. And you do the same' he said to me. 'You both have one week's leave. Collect your travel documents in the morning.'

It took us both most of the night getting our kit together and we were both excited, although I felt a little disappointed that I was not going to Hong Kong.

In the morning we said our goodbyes to the staff and shook hands with the colonel and other officers including our Staff Sergeant, who wished us good luck and told us to enjoy ourselves. Staff said Germany was a good posting and not to be too disappointed. There was little time to take it all in, as I was not expecting a posting so soon. Everything was moving too fast for any feeling except the need to get ready to go.

We collected our travel documents and leave passes, shook hands and travelled home. My family and girlfriend were surprised to see me. Telephones were not commonplace in 1954. They were not too happy that I had only a week and then was going away again for at least a year before I would see them again. I would only get two weeks' leave and a few days if lucky at Christmas.

The week went fast. My father got a taxi to Barking railway station, which was a treat. My mother, father, girlfriend and brother Peter travelled with me to Euston station to catch the train to Harwich. From Harwich a ship of the Royal Navy was to take me to the Hook of Holland. MPs were everywhere and embarkation was well disciplined. Many other soldiers of varied regiments and corps were off to Germany. We shuffled aboard via a gangplank and were told by a corporal which deck and berth we were to go to.

After descending two decks, I reached my berth. 'Right, move along laddie,' shouted a corporal, 'stow your gear.'

'Where?' I asked. I had a bunk amongst dozens in rows with some hammocks.

'Underneath the bottom bunk with the others' replied the corporal. Our gear was clearly labelled with full army number and name and posting, so it was safe enough.

The trip to the Hook of Holland was uneventful except that the sea became a little rough. I do not suffer from seasickness, but others did. After about half an hour the steel floor was running with vomit. The smell was unpleasant and was probably the cause of some stalwarts becoming sick as well as the original sufferers. Fortunately my bunk was in the middle of a tier of three. Those on the lower bunks and hammocks with the rolling of the ship were inches above the vomit. I and many other soldiers grabbed our kit just as the vomiting started and put it on our bunks. I spent most of the journey on the upper deck near the open hatch having a smoke. Others, however, just lay on their bunks amongst their gear and slept.

However the journey was somewhat boring. It would have been better if we could see where we were going, but all 'other ranks' were below decks.

Eventually we arrived at the Hook of Holland and orders were given to disembark. We collected and put on our gear and were told to stand by our bunks some amid the vomit. We stood for half an hour and some soldiers became agitated and vociferous. 'Silence in the ranks!' was shouted from above. We then heard the noise of metal studs on metal ladders and decks as men shuffled towards the gangplank, fresh air and the dockside. At the dockside all RAMC personnel were herded together and marched off in a column of two through the dockyard towards the railway station close by. Here our papers were checked and destinations called out at the request of the sergeant. I called out 'BMH Münster, sergeant'. No one else did. I was the only one destined for that part of Germany. Most of the soldiers were nursing orderlies and destined for Iserlohn, Hanover, Dortmund, Osnabruck, Wuppertal, Hamburg, Rinteln, Cologne and Berlin.

The journey was lively. Soldiers were playing poker and chess. Others were smoking, singing and telling jokes and seemed generally to be enjoying themselves. After about two hours we stopped at Essen, where some soldiers had to change trains for Cologne and Dusseldorf.

As we were pulling away from the station a soldier asked, 'Is this Essen?'

'Yeah' was the shout.

'Sod it' said the soldier, 'Come on Dave, we've got to change here.'

The train was gathering speed. They opened the carriage door and shouted to us to throw out their gear, then jumped off close to the end of the platform. We heaved their gear, including suitcases, out of the window and it bounced along the platform and off the end. Looking back we could see them gathering their bits and pieces together unharmed. In reply to our shouts they gave us a wave and a thumbs-up sign.

The passengers were now beginning to thin out and I began to start thinking about my destination. I had no idea where Münster Westfalen was and began reading the names of the stations we passed through. After about an hour we stopped at Hamm and I knew that the next major station would be Münster, according to the map on the carriage wall. I got my kit ready for departure and stood by the carriage door shouting 'Cheerio' to the lads in the carriage. As we came into the station I read the name, just in case. Yes it was Münster. This was it. As the train stopped I lobbed my gear out and climbed down onto the platform.

As the train pulled away the others in the carriage shouted 'Good luck mate!' 'The same to you!' I replied. I watched the train disappear standing surrounded by my kit bag, suitcase, greatcoat, backpack and waterproof cape.

I checked my breast pocket for my travel documents, loaded myself up with my gear and left the station. Outside I dumped my gear and immediately spotted a Redcap looking at me. 'Oh dear' I thought to myself, 'I hope I'm properly dressed.' He came up to me. 'You OK mate?' he asked. 'Yes' I replied, 'I'm posted to BMH Münster'.

'That's OK mate, someone will be along shortly to pick you up. Have a good journey.'

I was somewhat surprised. I did not expect that kind of treatment from the Military Police. I learnt during my eighteen months in Germany that the Redcaps were very helpful, unlike the officious attitudes in the UK. During that period Germany was still under military law and the German police were secondary to the military police.

Shortly a large army Humber drove up and a Quartermaster sergeant got out. He was tall and very friendly. 'Eldridge?' he enquired.

'Yes sir' I replied.'

'Not sir, just Q,' he said.

'Right Q' I said.

'Stow your gear in the back and sit next to me and I'll show you the town which you will get to know very well during your stay here.'

'Great' I replied.

He drove me all round the town, showing me the main restaurants, cafés and beer cellars. Münster is a cathedral and university town, but many of the buildings were still just shells. The town had suffered from the bombing during the war.

Driving towards the British Military Hospital adjoining the old Münster hospital I could see many bombed-out buildings but also many new modern buildings which were universities and colleges. The countryside was picturesque, with woods, streams and a lake, the Aa See.

When we arrived at the BMH, Q showed me around the cookhouse and then the NAAFI. He then took me to the Central Pathological Laboratories (the CPL) and introduced me to the staff, including the German civilian aides. The CPL supplied all other BMHs with blood transfusion and crystalloid equipment assembled in the laboratories and also supplied staff to go to other BMH's around Germany when a member of staff in the laboratories went on leave.

'Right' said Q, 'during the next month there will be others arriving. In the meantime this is your barrack room.' We had walked from the CPL for about fifty yards along a path to two long rectangular brick buildings. One building housed the cooks, the other was for the laboratory staff. It was divided into four sections, one being the showers, baths and hand basins, the other the toilets. A corridor ran down the centre of the building making two sleeping billets, ten beds in each with accompanying bedside cabinet and locker. These beds were along one wall opposite the corridor on the window side. On the floor space there was a table with about six chairs. A small room at the end contained ironing board, iron, brooms, mops and tins of reddish-brown polish to match the floor. There was one bed in the middle of the row window side, which was made up with boxed blankets and sheets etc. The rest were empty, just the bare slats.

At Millbank some of the beds had bamboo slats to hold the mattresses. One soldier I remember used to dive onto the bed at the end of his duty. One day he did this and the bamboo broke and he crashed through. Sitting up he shouted, 'Fuck this bambastard-boo' which made me laugh.

It was late afternoon and I was hungry. I went to the cookhouse, which was packed with soldiers in all states of dress, unbuttoned shirts, ties askew, no army boots, just black shoes. They all seemed happy. The meal was good but a lonely one. I retired to the NAAFI for a smoke and a couple of beers served by a German girl. There were two German girls behind the bar.

'Hello, just arrived?' asked one of the girls. 'Yes' I replied and gave them some money for a beer. 'You need to get some Deutsch marks or BAFS [British Armed Forces Currency] not English money. Don't worry, you can pay me next time I see you.'

'Thanks' I said.

'Do you speak any German?' the other girl asked.

'Just a couple of words' I said, 'like danke schön and bitte'.

'Well' said the girl, 'When you see us again say guten Tag, Morgen, Nacht or Abend. Elsa is my name, or I should say meine Name, and then say, 'wie gehts?' which means how are you, and we say 'gut dank, wie geht es Ihnen?' which means good, thank you and how are you.'

'Danke' I replied.

I stayed in the NAAFI for a while. It was very spacious and had a full-sized snooker table. The perimeter of the BMH and living and working areas was ringed with wire mesh fixed to high concrete posts topped with barbed wire. A couple of soldiers came up to me and told me that it was quite a good posting and was very relaxed. The morning parades were at 8 am and were quickly over, finishing about 8.15. You then went off to work.

I left the NAAFI and went back to my barrack room, made my bed and decided to call it a day. I was tired. I went for my ablutions. The toilets were very clean with gleaming tiles and mirrors. I found out they were cleaned regularly by a Polish cleaning woman. I washed, cleaned my teeth, switched out the lights, walked into the barrack room, undressed and lay down on my bed, thinking about the events of the day.

I had never felt such loneliness in my life. I was alone in a barrack room with nine other empty beds. Across the corridor the adjoining barrack room was also very quiet. The residents were probably still in the NAAFI. Whether it was the combination of tiredness and being far from home I don't know, but I had a little cry. I had been on my own all the way from Harwich apart from others on the journey who appeared to have company all the way to their postings.

I was awakened at 7 am by the duty corporal. 'OK lad' he said, 'Breakfast is at 7.30 am and parade at 8 am.'

'Where?' I asked.

'In front of the reception main entrance to the hospital' he replied.

Breakfast was fine. I felt better. I met the other laboratory staff, and found that they were billeted in the next barrack room.

A Path Lab corporal told me there were two parades, one outside reception with the other hospital staff and ours, which was outside the Central Pathology building. The reason I was told was because we were not part of BMH Münster, the Central Pathology Service being a separate unit. The CO BMH Münster, a major, did not have jurisdiction over us. We were accountable to our CO, who was a colonel. 'Sounds good' I said. 'Yes' said the corporal.

The main parade was a bit of a shambles with just the rudimentary line up, coming to attention for a quick inspection and then dismissed by a smart RSM with a dapper waxed moustache. No gaiters or boots, just our shoes, well-polished of course. The Central Pathology Laboratory (CPL) parade was similar only quicker.

After the CPL parade I was introduced to the lab staff by Q and shook hands with the colonel and other officers. Yes, I shook hands!

'Well' said the colonel, 'Welcome to CPL. All departments are fully staffed at the moment. Spend a day or two in each department. Get to know everyone and what is expected of you and then I want you to work with the corporal in charge of the crystalloids department.'

This department was large, making blood transfusion kits and bottles of sterile saline and sterile glucose and citrate bottles for blood collection to be used for transfusion. There was not a store of blood for transfusion. When someone needed blood, then a soldier with the right blood group would be sent for and a pint taken from him in exchange for a bottle of Guinness. I found out very soon that they were given a cup of tea and the Guinness was stored for parties etc.

There was a large sterilisation room with large ovens and autoclaves. In this room a couple of German workers were employed. One was a girl about twenty-plus years who told us she preferred us 'Tommies' because she had been raped a couple of times near Berlin when the 'Yanks' came in. The other worker was a man, somewhat older. There was another man who was our driver. He picked up and delivered blood transfusion bottles and equipment to the railway station for other BMH hospitals of the British Armies On the Rhine (BAOR) throughout Germany in a large army Humber. He knew London quite well but from the air. He had flown Messerschmitts during the war.

After a week in all departments, including the animal house with mainly guinea pigs and rabbits with a few sheep in the adjoining field, I settled in the crystalloid department. After a week of this I began to enjoy it. The transfusion kits were prepared with needles sharpened and capped, the rubber tubing assembled and curled and wrapped in Cellophane ready for steam sterilisation in the autoclaves. They were wrapped in a special way to allow for shrinkage of the Cellophane but result in a tightly sealed package. After sterilisation they were inspected for any splits as were the bottles of crystalloid solutions. Each bottle was held up after sterilisation and cooling against a black background with a light shining through the bottle. Any 'bits' or cloudiness observed and the bottle was rejected.

After two weeks my barrack room began to fill up. Some of the laboratory staff were being demobbed and new staff replacements were arriving. Each double barrack room with a corridor down the middle held twenty soldiers.

Wednesdays was sports day – for some. Some used it for a lie in, others played snooker in the NAAFI. I joined the rugby union team organised by our colonel, and also the cricket team. I began training with others from the laboratory plus a Corporal cook from the catering corps. Some officers from the BMH were also training, and some nursing orderlies.

We had a match every two weeks, not against just other BMHs in the BAOR area but also other regiments and corps. This was most enjoyable, as I travelled to matches around Germany playing rugby. I started as prop but although fit I was not really big enough. Our hooker was a Scot and being small in a scrum his feet dangled in the air. I was twelve stone and given the position of flanker.

Bert, a Scot from Perth and a biochemist in the laboratory, was our scrum half. He was about five foot four and almost as wide and covered in dark hair like a gorilla suffering from a mild form of alopecia. He was a good biochemist and a good scrum half, being very strong.

In one game against a tank regiment he collected the ball from the scrum and instead of passing it out decided to run with it. The opposing scrum half saw him and went for him. Bert was running in a crouched attitude and as the tackler went for him both heads collided. Bert dropped the ball and was laid flat out, but came to after about ten seconds. The tackler was carried off on a stretcher and did not regain consciousness for at least ten minutes. Bert carried on as if nothing had happened. I don't think he even had a headache.

I was not always able to play because on some Wednesdays I was on call at the laboratory and we had to sleep there. It was hardly ever busy. Sometimes we were accepting a delivery of vaccines or blood to be cross-matched or some biochemical analyses.

After a month in the crystalloid department the corporal in charge was demobbed. I was sent to see the colonel. There were another couple of soldiers in the department but they were not laboratory trained and so were only laboratory assistants.

When we reached the colonel's door, Q said 'Smarten up a bit Brian and stand by the door and let's have a little bit of bull please' He knocked. 'Come in.' He opened the door, came to attention and said 'Sir, 809 Eldridge reporting sir'. I marched through the door and came to attention.

'Er, stand at ease please' said the colonel. 'Your corporal is being demobbed. You have been in the department for a month now and I have been told that you have become very proficient with all the disciplines involved. I want you to take charge of the department. You will be made up to full corporal immediately. As you know it is a very responsible position supplying the whole of the BAOR.'

All I could say was 'Thank you sir'. I was speechless.

'Right Q. Off you go and get his corporal stripes sewn on. You will still be required to do on call duties and also take the morning CPL parades.'

Off we went. Q with a smile said 'Not bad going laddie'. I would be privy to the corporal's mess, a special room and bar in the NAAFI.

In the first week I organised the department so that production could be increased. We were always hard pushed to keep up with requests of transfusion sets and bottles. The following week new recruits arrived, and he was given an extra person. A Scot from Edinburgh arrived who was put in charge of haematology and made up to full corporal. They were all billeted with me. That gave two full corporals in my barrack room. We became great friends. He sported a ginger moustache similar to the RSM's. Whenever possible we went into town together.

In the crystalloid department large gallon jars with handles at the neck were filled with normal saline. A rubber bung in the neck was fitted with three tubes, one from a pressure pump, one to deliver the saline to the transfusion bottles and one with a clip to regulate the pressure. The jar was enclosed in a wooden box in case under pressure it exploded. When a bottle had the required amount of saline, it was exchanged for an empty one and so on. Unfortunately the pressure usually blew out the bung, so it had to be wired down and transfusion needles stuck into the tubing helped to keep the pressure down. You had to be attentive all the time. We wore rubber boots and long post mortem gowns and I managed to get duck boards for the stone floor to prevent slipping.

It was during a run that we had an inspection from one of the BMH officers who was somewhat officious. The pump was chugging away and the jar was under pressure. Q came in shouting 'Attention, officer's inspection. Corporal on your feet.'

'I can't Q,' I replied. 'The jar is under pressure and it might blow and I do not want to halt the production line'.

'On your feet corporal!' said the officer.

'I can't. The jar will blow if I don't watch it' I said loudly.

'Put that man on a charge, Q,' ordered the officer. The officer proceeded to inspect the production line and I stood to one side at attention with the other staff. As he approached the pump area it blew with a bang. The bung flew off the jar, splitting the protection box and throwing saline over all of us and in particular the officer. I looked at him with what would be termed in the army as dumb insolence. The officer quickly left.

Q came back half an hour later after having a word with our colonel and said the charge had been dropped. This I took as an apology. I have seen soldiers put on a charge for dumb insolence. When being shouted at by a sergeant or criticised by an officer you only have to raise an eyebrow, literally, and this is construed as insolence.

Weekends were usually free unless you were on on-call duty. We usually went into town, especially when there was one of the many German festival holidays like the Rosenmontagfest or the Oktoberfest, or other beer festivals. This was a reason to order more German marks with your pay instead of BAFS. It was on pay parades that one noticed the different ways that cooks, RASC (Royal Army Service Corps) and other corps saluted and how they wore their berets. Cooks' berets were worn not with the badge over the left eye with the right side pulled down to the right ear, but had the badge dead centre and both sides pulled down. Some had their berets shrunk by boiling and some pulled the front down just above the eyebrows. Ties were also boiled, to change the colour. Their salutes were equally exaggerated. Some flourished the open right hand quivering behind their heads. With the RASC the hand went up with fingers pointing to the sky and not at right angles as per Queen's Regulations.

We usually caught a bus into town, buying a Fahrscheinerheft, which was a book of tickets. We started off visiting a Bierkeller where our usual meal was Wienerschnitzel mit zwei Spiegeleier und Kartoffelsalat (pork covered with two fried eggs and potato salad). This was followed with schnapps and beer chasers. It was very rare to get back to the BMH sober. We had to book out of camp and book back in so that the duty officer knew if any one was AWOL (absent without leave). To book in it was very important to straighten your shoulders and not say too much but sign in. If you were thought to be drunk you were put on a charge.

One night five of us, after returning from a birthday celebration, went straight to the NAAFI after booking in at the curfew time of eleven. We bought some whisky, and things started to get a little out of hand. We 'borrowed' the camp's fire ladder, which was one of the telescopic types with ratchet and winding handle. It had two large wooden wheels with spokes and a 'T' bar for pulling. Moustachioed Dick with a glass of scotch in his hand was wound up the ladder to about forty feet by two of us on the winding handle. He stood at the top singing at the top of his voice. 'She was on the bridge at midnight throwing snowballs at the moon and she said she'd never had it but she spoke too fucking soon.' A rendering from which song I cannot remember. This commotion brought out the duty officer and duty sergeant. 'Get down from there man!' shouted the officer. We were all in civvies, so the duty officer did not know who we were or where we were from in the BMH.

Dick took no notice. The sergeant bellowed at him. Dick undid his flies and pissed over the sergeant and officer, oblivious to what was happening below. 'Right' said the sergeant, and he kicked the ratchet away holding the ladder up. Dick came down fast, still standing on the ladder rungs. He had not spilt a drop of whisky from his glass. We were ordered to return the ladder to the fire compound and report to reception. We returned the ladder but did not report to reception. We heard nothing about the incident or failing to report, which was a puzzle. Perhaps it was too embarrassing for people to know you had been pissed on from a great height.

After one trip into town we returned to find the rest of the barrack room crew a bit merry. The technician on duty had been requested to analyse some rum from the sergeant's mess of a tank regiment. Someone was accused of watering it down.

'How much do you require?' the technician was asked. 'We need the whole bottle I'm afraid, 'replied the technician. The bottle in question was half a gallon in a wicker casing. The usual 100 cc was taken out of the bottle for analysis and found to be OK and reported to the tank regiment. The rest was in the barrack room being consumed.

We gave them some help and started singing to music from our radio on the Luxembourg wavelength. We had a late-night early-morning session. Incidentally the radio was passed from barrack room to barrack room if they could afford a licence. We, however, never seemed to be without it.

Unfortunately we were in a poor state for morning parade. One of the lads had to be supported between Dick and me to stop him swaying. It was noticed by the RSM, and the whole of the CPL staff, who had obviously dressed hastily and had hangovers, were put on a charge and were to report to reception on defaulters' parade at 6 pm in best BD (battle dress). After our day's work the lab staff who were on a charge, which was most of us except the one who was on call, filed out of the laboratory. We had a quick evening meal and dashed back to the barrack room to bull up and get changed for inspection outside reception at 6 pm.

We were sixteen in number and being the senior corporal now that the other corporals had been demobbed, I marched them out in columns of two. Waiting for us was the RSM and two sergeants. 'Path lab halt!' I shouted. 'Front rank right face. Rear rank forward march.' When the rear rank reached the last man in the front rank, I halted them. Then 'Right face' and then 'One pace forward march.' I was getting them in single file with quizzical looks from the sergeants and a smile from the RSM.

'Right dress,' I ordered. Right arms were raised to the next soldier's shoulder and shuffled to get the line straight. This done, I then called 'Stand at ease'. We were now in one straight line ready for inspection. The RSM and both sergeants came down the reception steps.

'Well lads, you look a lot better' said the RSM. 'I'm not sure about the drill commands though.' The three inspected us but found little fault except one of us did not come to attention when confronted by the RSM. 'Good' he said. 'Let's not have another situation like we had this morning. Right corporal, march them off.'

'Path lab attention. Right turn.' I was now stumped. How could I get them back in two ranks to march them off? The middle man, number eight, was a Welshman named Jones. So without hesitation I shouted 'From Jones slightly to the left quick march.' When he reached the front man I shouted 'Halt!' Then 'Path lab by the left quick march'.

'Wait a minute!' shouted the RSM. 'That's not in the drill manual! "From Jones slightly to the left?"' I halted them. The sergeants were laughing. 'We think it should be added.' said one. 'OK' said the RSM, 'bugger off'. Off we marched with bags of swank, all grinning except Dick, the other corporal, who was guffawing out loud and shouting 'In a pig's eye', a common phrase of his.

Two weeks later Dick and I were summoned by Q and told to prepare an officer's wife who had died the previous week for a funeral and burial in the grounds close to the chapel.

We arrived at the small chapel, which was littered with leaves. We swept out the chapel and lifted the coffin onto the trestles, screwed the lid down as it was loose, and started to drape the union flag over the coffin. 'Right' I said, 'Let's have a smoke.' The procession and ceremony were not due for another hour so we had a smoke and a lie down in the grass. A little skive was very acceptable.

After about fifteen minutes a corporal from the hospital reception about a quarter of a mile away walked over to us from a car parked in the small road by the chapel.

'Everything OK corporals?' he said.

'Yes' I replied.

'Any trouble finding the body?' he asked.

'What?' said Dick. 'What do you mean?' the corporal's eyes widened. 'Didn't you get the body from the morgue over at the hospital?'

'Shit, no,' I said.

'Right,' said the corporal, 'you go for the body and I'll dash back and get an ambulance and meet you at the mortuary. Fuck me we've only got forty- five minutes before they get here with the whole fucking church parade.'

Off we ran. Dick had got the name and number of the officer's wife. 'I thought the coffin was a bit light when we lifted it' said Dick, 'But I came to the conclusion she was small and very thin.'

We dashed down to the mortuary in the hospital cellars and found the refrigerated tray with the number and name of the officer's wife. We lifted her out and placed her onto a trolley, then pushed her up the ramp to the road outside where the ambulance was waiting and eager to get going. We lifted the body on board and off we went, fast. It took just a couple of minutes in the ambulance. We now had just twenty-five minutes. We unscrewed the coffin, lowered the shrouded body in and screwed it down again. Then we carefully covered the coffin with the union flag. The ambulance sped off. We also sped off at a run, because fifty yards away we could see the procession headed by the army chaplain coming down the path.

On the way back to the laboratory we met Q. 'Everything OK lads?' he asked.

'Oh yes' we replied, 'no sweat'. In fact the sweat was running down our faces. We went back to the barrack room before our evening meal. 'Christ' said Dick, 'they nearly had a service over an empty coffin.' I said, 'The body might have stayed in the mortuary for years'. This released the stress and we collapsed laughing. 'Aye fucking aye' spluttered Dick. I think we could have been court-martialled, but I did not enquire if it was a court martial offence because questions would have been asked.

That was not the only experience we had with bodies.

That winter of 1955 was quite severe in Münster. After Christmas it snowed heavily and it was very cold. The snow was over two feet deep and the drifts over four. We had spectacular snowball fights in the evenings after duty with twenty to thirty soldiers battling on the playing fields. In town the local children and adults tobogganed down the hills surrounding the Aa See the local lake.

'Corporal, get someone to help you bring a sergeant from the hospital mortuary for a post mortem,' said Q. 'Yes Q' I said. I called Dick, who was with me for the officer's wife's funeral and another from the laboratory staff. We collected the shrouded body from the ward on a trolley and wheeled it from the hospital along the pathways to the mortuary. Unfortunately we hit a hidden hole in the icy path, which broke one of the wheels. The force of the impact shot the body off the trolley into the snow at the side of the path. The drifted and shovelled snow was about two feet higher than the surrounding snow-covered fields. We could not see the white shrouded body in the snow, and even searching around the hole it had made was not fruitful. We scrabbled around for about five minutes scooping snow away with our hands but still no luck.

We sent the other laboratory technician to go back to the barrack room and get a couple of extra hands to help. The five of us spent nearly half an hour searching anxiously until we finally found the body. It had slid down the slope at the side of the path and continued on the ice and snow until it ended up under a bench near one of the flowerbeds. It was only noticed after considerable digging by George, one of the extras, because he saw a tattooed arm sticking out from the bench seat. I had embarrassing visions of the whole army camp searching in the snow and reprimands for us two corporals. We eventually got the body back intact to the mortuary. The only comment that was made by the captain doing the post mortem was to ask why the body was so wet.

During this cold snowy weather Dick and a couple of other soldiers slept in their beds with the windows at the head of the beds wide open. They loved fresh air. One morning during a blizzard we awoke to find them fast asleep but covered in inches of snow except where they were breathing, which was just a wet patch. They occasionally filled a bath with cold water and immersed themselves. I gave it a try, but only once.

That Christmas I flew home for two weeks' leave. It was great being a civilian again but difficult to adjust. I stubbed my cigarettes out in the saucer or teacup. I also included occasionally extra adjectives like, 'The turkey's fucking good mum. Oops sorry mum.' There were raised eyebrows from the family, but after a day or two I had control and was back to normal.

The two weeks soon passed and I was once again on my way to Harwich to get the boat to Hook of Holland. I had hoped to fly back – the reason why I travelled back by train and ship I never found out. The army works in mysterious ways. However I was approached by a military police sergeant. 'Corporal, are you en route to Germany?'

'Yes sarge' I replied.

'Follow me then.' I was marched to the front of a desk by the platform entrance where a military police officer was seated. 'Corporal, your travel documents please.'

I handed them over.

'Right corporal, you'll do' he said. 'You are to escort a prisoner to the Hook of Holland and hand him over to the military police there. He is AWOL from the 10th Lancers. Is that understood?'

'Yes' I replied.

'You choose another soldier to assist you and report back to me'.

I saluted and left. Fortunately a Nursing Orderly class 3 from Münster was also on the platform. I had been chatting to him earlier.

'Hi, Alan, I've a job for you,' I said. I told him what was up and he followed me back to the MP officer, a major. We saluted and Alan handed over his travel documents. I then signed a paper putting me in charge of the AWOL lancer. The lancer was marched from a railway guard office by the sergeant and told he was in my charge. It was then that I was handed a white MP's belt and holster occupied by a large revolver with lanyard.

'Excuse me sir,' I said to the major, 'I am RAMC and a non-combatant, therefore I am not happy with this sidearm'.

'The prisoner and the sidearm are signed over to you corporal and you are now responsible for him and the pistol. It is fully loaded and is for your protection if there is any trouble. I assure you there will be none.'

I felt a little conspicuous with the holster bouncing against my hip. I still do not understand why they could not spare or afford a military policeman as an escort to the Hook.

The journey to Harwich was without incident. The prisoner, David, was friendly but understandably not very talkative. Apparently he was having trouble with his fiancée and did not want to go back to his unit with his problems unsolved. He would probably get a few weeks or more in the 'glasshouse'.

Boarding the ship at Harwich was great. The MP's gave us priority and choice of bunks close to the upper deck. Customs and document formalities were waived. I was beginning to like this.

On board we kept a good eye on the prisoner but there was not any trouble, as he couldn't go anywhere. He was accompanied to ablutions etc by one of us. Anything he wanted or wished to purchase we got for him. He stayed mainly in his bunk. There were no hammocks this time.

The crossing was smooth and disembarkation easy. We were off the ship first and went immediately to the MP offices. I handed over the prisoner, wished him good luck and shook his hand. I said 'cheerio' to the MP corporal and started to make my way with Alan, my assistant, to the station to catch the train to Münster.

'Oy Corp!' The MP was running after me.

'What's up?' I asked.

'You don't really look like John Wayne,' he said.

'Christ, it's surprising how quickly you get used to things' I answered. I unbuckled the belt, handed the heavy weapon over to the corporal, signed the papers and left for Münster Westfalen.

I was to be reminded of this incident during my demob. We had to relinquish most of our kit and it was ticked off as you threw it on the growing pile. We had to keep some, especially those that were Army Emergency Reserve (AER). We remained on AER for three years after demob.

Noticeable was the pile of boots. Most of the boots were being lobbed over the pile and then being retrieved by the soldiers as they walked out of the marquee. It was difficult to throw a comfortable pair of boots away, so the boot pile did not grow very fast.

However as I was leaving after signing the necessary papers I was called to come back by a sergeant. 'Where's the revolver issued to you?' I explained that it had been handed over and signed for. He would not have it. I knew the sergeant well, but did not like him much. Fortunately amongst my documents I still had a copy of the MP's document. The sergeant reluctantly dismissed me.

That February we had a newcomer. He was seconded to us from the Royal Canadian Army Medical Corps stationed in Soest with their Pioneer Corps and Service Corps. Soest was a small town also occupied by the Belgian Army. As we were the Central Pathology Laboratory we did most of the blood tests for that region, especially Wasserman Reaction (WR) tests for syphilis. The Canadians were responsible for a high percentage of the total workload, so they sent us a laboratory technician to help us out. He was a corporal about six foot two inches tall and huge all round. He wore regulation wire spectacles and was untidy in his

Canadian uniform, which was of much better quality than ours. It was lighter in weight and darker khaki. The boots he wore were long and high sided, negating the use of gaiters.

He arrived in the barrack room in the evening, after our evening meal. He dumped his kit on the floor and stood rather ill at ease as the men in the barrack room looked at him silently. I walked up to him, told him my name and shook his hand, which was twice the size of mine. 'Glad to know you, corp,' he said with a big grin. 'My name is Corporal John Simmons but you can just call me 'Moose'.' This was definitely an appropriate name for him.

'Is there somewhere I can get some chow?' he asked.

'My name's Brian' I said, 'and this is Dick' introducing my Scots 'mucker'.' I told him the only place at this time of the evening was the NAAFI. 'Great' he said. We took him there and he bought some German sausage, bread and a few beers. 'This is a bit embarrassing,' he said. 'I've got a couple of dollars and my pay does not come through until the end of the week. Can I get a loan from any of you guys? I'll write you out an IOU.' Dick volunteered with £2 pounds of BAFS and I with £1.

'OK' he said with relish, 'Now we can get started.' He went up to the NAAFI counter, handed over some German marks and £2 of BAFS and got two crates of Dortmunder beer, that is twenty-four bottles. Five of us sat around a table drinking beer and smoking and getting to know Moose and the Canadian army. He was to stay with us for three months until the backlog of blood tests was cleared. Then we should have another man joining our team.

The CPL also had to send men to other German cities that had a BMH when they were sent on leave or demobbed. During my time I was sent to Berlin and Hamburg for a week each. Dick was sent to Berlin, Hamburg and Rinteln. Others were sent to Hanover and Cologne.

I asked Moose if his speciality was in virology and in particular venereal diseases. 'Yes' he said. 'The French Canadian Pioneer Corps keeps us busy.'

'So you are OK with our techniques then?' I asked.

'Oh yeah' he said, 'We no longer throw the blood specimen against the wall.'

'What?' I said.

'Well' said Moose, 'if it sticks the guy's got the clap, if it slides down the wall he ain't got the clap.'

The three months he was with us were a breath of fresh air. At the end of the week he got paid in Canadian dollars, which he changed to US dollars for a better rate of exchange (I think it was that way round) and German marks. He paid us back the money he owed. We got paid about £10 per month. He got paid about £50, in his words just to piss against the wall. He thanked us by taking us into Münster and buying us a slap-up meal and all the beer we could drink. We enjoyed his company.

On parade he stood out like a sore thumb. It was not so much his size but his different uniform. One weekend we had a special parade because the CO of the Canadian Army in Soest was to visit and inspect us, a French Canadian. He was also to inspect the laboratories, so I think the presence of Moose was the reason and he was curious to see how he was settling in. He was a Brigadier but not RCAMC. He wore a Sam Brown leather belt and straps with ribbons on his left breast. Very smart!

On parade he inspected us and stopped in front of Moose and spoke to him in French. Moose replied in a hesitant French. The officer stiffened and turned to his accompanying NCO. The NCO immediately spoke to our RSM, who sent Moose off accompanied by two sergeants to the guardroom. With our colonel's intervention he did not stay in the guardroom long, he was released almost immediately. He had important work to do.

I learnt afterwards that the officer had said to Moose that his belt was dirty, that he was untidy and not properly fixed. Moose had replied that it was better than the boy-scout outfit the officer had on. The officer had been insulted. Moose got two days CB (confined to barracks).

We went out that weekend for a booze-up. 'I thought you would have had at least a week in CB' I said. 'Well' said Moose, 'Your colonel and mine back at Soest want the WRs done so I was let off lightly. Your colonel thought it was funny.'

During our booze-up Moose invited us back to his camp for a visit the following weekend, starting on Friday after duty. Dick and I were free but the others were tied down with duties or had other things planned. We obtained leave passes and that Friday travelled to Soest. We immediately went to corps reception, where a major was sitting at a desk. Dick and I came to attention, although we were in civvies.

'Hey Joe' said Moose, shaking the major by the hand, 'meet a couple of my buddies from Münster. Can you find them a couple of beds and get someone to get some bedding for them please?'

'OK Moose' said the major, 'Have a good time.'

The informality between officers and men was a little strange to us. We dumped our gear in the barrack room lockers, then walked into town. The first stop was the Toc H for a cup of coffee. Toc H is a society originally of ex-servicemen founded after the First World War to promote Christian and social service. Toc is the old telegraphy code for T and the H is for house, from Talbot House, a soldier's club in Belgium in 1915.

During coffee we decided to have a meal in the NAAFI and then go into town and visit a few Bierkellers. The NAAFI in the Canadian camp was huge. We were introduced to a couple of French Canadian infantrymen and they decided to tag along with us. One of them, called Boussière, bought us dinner, barbecued spare ribs and fried eggs. I had never had spare ribs before and I had more than I could manage on my plate. We finished and retired to another part of the NAAFI where they had snooker tables and a small dance floor. There were Canadian nurses and the equivalent of our WRACS (Women's Royal Army Corps) dancing with some men and with each other. We had a great time and got rather drunk.

On the way back to camp we walked through the guardroom gates, where two lorries were parked. Boussière turned to me and said 'Un moment s'il vous plait Monsieur Brian, there is someone I wish to say Bonjour to.'

Boussière walked over to the cabin of the lorry and opened the door, where a driver, probably on duty, was asleep. He stepped up on the running board and smashed his fist into the driver's face. Then he calmly stepped down and walked with us to the barrack room.

'Er… what was that all about?' asked Dick.

'Well you see,' said Boussière, 'he owes me a little money but will not pay me back. I sink I will now let him keep it, n'est ce pas?'

The French Canadian infantry, especially the Pioneer Corps, were a rough lot and enjoyed an occasional fight, explained Moose. We saw some the following evening on parade. A high percentage of them wore beards or huge moustaches and most were in need of a haircut. Moose and the French Canadians took us into town after our breakfast. The army food was an eye opener and very different from our army grub. They had pickles on the table with various sauces and choices of cereals. We could have meats, ham, eggs, toast, coffee or tea. This was a nice change from our greasy bacon and eggs and a mug of dark brown tea. Their laid-back attitude to their officers was also quite refreshing.

Moose took us to a few 'pubs' filled mostly with Canadian soldiers. There was a Belgian contingent stationed in Soest, but they were not seen in the pubs. I asked Moose about this and

I was told that they got about a penny a day in comparison to Moose's pay so they could not afford the luxury and were not allowed to go out in civvies.

'Just as well' said Moose, 'there's enough fights among the pioneer corps as it is.'

We had a great time, and on the train back to Münster we decided to have a long weekend next month including Moose and take a trip down the river Mosel. There were three of us on this trip; another two would meet us in Bernkastel.

The train journey was not without incident. The train was delayed for about half an hour for some reason, so we started to drink some brandy that Moose had bought. The train guard sat with us and in a mixture of German and English asked us where we were going and where we had come from. He began to help us with the brandy. We exchanged life histories with difficulty. Apparently he had been imprisoned by the Russians for about a year and it took us about twenty minutes to find out that he did not comprehend the word 'prison' and in the end the word 'gaol' saved the situation. He looked at his watch and said 'Mein Gott, I am about to start the Zug [train] yah?' He had a consultation with another official on the platform and after two minutes blew his whistle and waved his flag and as we started to move and pick up speed he was still waving it. We passed him as the train gathered speed. Our carriage was the last next to the guards van. Moose stuck his head out of the window. The guard saw him, realising that now the train was going faster than he thought. The guards van had already passed him and he began to run. He started to gain on the train but not by much. I thought he was going to be left behind. We started to shout encouragement, which urged him to a greater effort. Dick opened our door. He was level with the guards van, but it was closed. Seeing Moose with his hand outstretched he made a beeline for us. Moose grabbed him and yanked him into the carriage. Dick grabbed his flag. We picked him up gasping from the floor between the seats, sat him down and gave him some brandy. 'Danke' he spluttered. 'Bitte' we chorused, which made him laugh.

'I sink dat ve haf perhaps genug ja?' he said, laughing but swallowed another mouthful anyway. At the next stop he got out and went back to his guards van. He whistled and got the train going again but did not join us this time. When we reached Bernkastel we said our goodbyes and proceeded into town. Across the river over a stone bridge is another town called Cochem. In Bernkastel we started to look for lodgings, Fremdenzimmer. We found lodgings, although it was one room with two large beds and a very heavy duvet. This was the first time I had seen this sort of bed covering – sheets and blankets only in my experience. We dumped our gear and headed into town.

Graham and Ian were to meet us in Bernkastel, and after several stops at the many pubs we saw them in the town square. We told them where we were lodging and arranged to meet them back in the square. We all then went to a large Bierkeller with music being played. They were a quartet with two on accordions. We had a great time with lots of beer and German sausage. The beers were served in large steins carried three, sometimes four, in each hand by buxom waitresses. I was amazed how they could carry so many, but looking at their arms you could see that they were very muscular.

The tables had stone vases with large bunches of gladioli in them. After a while I noticed that the gladioli were slowly diminishing. The stems were still there, but the blooms were missing. Ian nudged me and pointed to a moustachioed German of about forty who was picking the blooms off and eating them. He saw me looking and said 'Sehr gut mit Salat' and laughed. I tried one but was not impressed.

The trip back to our Fremdenzimmer was noisy with singing, and then we reached the river Mosel and started to cross the bridge. It was a double arched stone bridge about twenty feet high with sides about four feet high and a couple of feet wide. There were four of us. Graham was missing. Where he had got to we had no idea. The last we saw of him he had been chatting to a Fräulein.

Moose climbed onto the bridge wall and started to cross, balancing precariously and singing. 'Careful' shouted Ian, laughing. However we all followed Moose. When he got to the centre of the bridge he threw his hands in the air and shouting 'Geronimo!' then leapt off the bridge and hit the water with a great splash. He quickly rose to the surface, spluttering and shouting 'Come on you guys, it's great!' We did. The water was not that deep for I touched bottom quickly, and it took only a few strokes to reach the sloping stony bank. We got to the Fremdenzimmer laughing and soaked to the skin and knocked on the door, because Graham had the key. The man of the house came to the door, looked us up and down, smiled, pointed to our shoes and indicated that we should remove them along with our socks. With hands on hips he called to his wife, who burst out laughing and started to peel the clothes off some of us. The rest of us took the hint and stripped down to our underpants. She hung them in front of a large stove, on the backs of chairs and on lines. We were then given towels and hot coffee. The man said 'Wo ist der andere Freund?' (Where is your other friend?)

'Christ' said Dick, 'I had forgotten about Graham'. We shrugged. An hour later, as we were preparing for bed, we heard the man of the house open the front door. We looked out of the window and there was Graham staggering past the door. The man stuck his arm out and grabbed Graham by the collar, and with one yank hauled him into the house. Graham however was not wet. 'Fucking hell, watcha want?' shouted Graham 'Cooker' said the man and pointed to our clothes in front of the stove. We were watching now from the stairs. 'Ah' said Graham, 'Danke schön mein Herr' and bowed. He would still be walking up the road if the man had not waited up for him. He then followed us up the stairs.

'Gute Nacht' we called. 'Gute Nacht' replied the man, laughing. Moose called out, 'That's what I call hospi-bloody-tality'.

We slept well packed into two beds with the heavy duvet, but in the morning we were suffering a little. We went down to breakfast, but before solids we were given tomato juice with a copious amount of Worcestershire sauce and some schnapps poured in. It was a real pick-me-up for our hangovers. We had cereals and then ham with Pumpernickel bread.

We left afterwards and paid the woman extra money for her trouble. She tried to refuse, but Moose, towering over the little woman, grabbed her hand and folded the marks into her palm and gave her a kiss. She smiled and accepted. They surprisingly gave us fond farewells, probably relieved to get rid of us.

After this we made our way to Cochem for a couple of days. We had heard that there was a town festival there. All there is to say is that we ate well, drank well and had a great time. My time in the army was passing quickly. We worked hard during the day and at night when we had the money we were either in the NAAFI or in town.

Alan, one of my staff in the crystalloids department, had his two front teeth removed because they were broken when he got too close to a lamp-post one night. The army dentist fitted him with some crowns. He was very pleased and we decided to go into town. He had met a German girl the previous weekend and had arranged to meet her and treat her to a meal at the Altes Leve, a Bierkeller well known to BMH personnel. Dick and I volunteered to escort Alan, as he was a little nervous. We caught a bus outside the BMH after buying cheese rolls from the NAAFI.

We did not have much money and decided not to have too much to eat at the Bierkeller and save it to spend on the Fräulein.

The bus was crowded and we stood by the doorway. I started eating my roll, as did Dick. Alan took a bite out of his roll and I was going to ask him if he was going to take the girl to the same place we were going when I noticed the cheese roll in his hand. It had two teeth stuck in it where he had taken a bite. Alan was unaware. They could not have been well fixed. The cheese in the roll must have gripped them.

I looked at Alan with astonishment and then with laughter as Dick also noticed. The dismay on his face when he realised he had a gap in his mouth was hilarious. He decided that he could not face the girl he was to meet. The people on the crowded bus also seemed amused.

'Can you put them back?' I asked. He tried. 'No fuck it, the stems or whatever they use seemed to have snapped. Bastards.'

'Well' said Dick, 'I suppose we'll have to put up with you then.'

'Can you see the girl for me and say I couldn't make it?' Alan asked Dick.

'What is she like?' asked Dick. 'She's a blonde,' Alan replied.

'Aye all right' said Dick, 'but it'll cost you a pint and a couple of Schnapps'.

We got off the bus, Alan with his teeth in his pocket. We went to the Altes Leve Gasthaus whilst Dick met the girl, Sigrid, at another Gasthaus two minutes away.

After about an hour and a half Alan was not looking pleased. Dick turned up about fifteen minutes later. 'You took your bloody time!' Alan accused Dick.

'You canna fucking well tell the girl what happened and then bugger off can you?' said Dick. 'I bought her a couple of drinks and had a meal. She wasnae too bad either,' he grinned. 'Too good for you, you toothless bugger. Anyway you owe me for a couple of Schnapps as promised and a Schnitzel and chips and a couple of Liebfraumilch that she had.'

Alan got up to buy. 'Brian' whispered Dick, 'Don't ye say anything but I've arranged to meet her next weekend.'

We all had a good time and on the way back to barracks Alan asked, 'Did she say when I was to see her again?'

'No' said Dick, 'she decided she wasna interested anymore.'

'Oh' said Alan. 'Ah well, never mind.'

Dick did meet her that weekend but it was the only time. He was more interested in one of the QARANC nurses (Queen Alexander Royal Army Medical Corps).

Another Brian in our barrack room always received food parcels from home, as we all did occasionally, but his was every other week. He always had about a dozen apples, apart from lots of other goodies like sweets, cigarettes, cakes, biscuits and money. We always shared our food parcels with the others except the cigarettes, clothing and money. However Brian never did share. He used to open his parcel at night after lights out. We could hear the rustling of paper and the munching of biscuits. A few rude comments were made but it made little difference. The apples he received would always be lined up in a row on his locker shelf.

One night when he was on duty we picked his lock and ate all his apples down to the core and then replaced them in a row back on the locker shelf and snapped the padlock shut again. When he came back in again about midnight the lights were out and we were all in bed feigning sleep. We heard the key turn in his padlock and the squeak of the locker door opening. There was a rustling of paper and the munching of biscuits. There was a long pause and then, 'What the...' another pause and 'You fucking bastards I'll 'ave you, the lot of you!' The barrack room was in muffled uproar with our laughter under the bedclothes.

He was a bit of a loner and because of this was often picked on. He spent most of his spare time building model railway trucks. They were very good, but it is important to mix with everyone you are barracked with to get on in the army. He was odd in other ways too, for example he slept with his eyes and mouth wide open. During the summer months the barrack room was usually full of moths and crane flies from the surrounding fields, attracted by our lights. We normally dispatched them with rubber tubing from the transfusion department. The tubing was pulled back as with a catapult and when released it splattered the moths against the wall. This had to be cleaned in the morning before inspection. Some of these moths were caught alive at night and placed on Brian's bottom lip whilst he slept. Bets were placed on how far the moth could crawl without wakening him. It was 20 to 1 if the moth crawled in his mouth and 100 to 1 if he swallowed it. This he never did. He usually coughed the moth out before it reached that far.

One or two other men in the laboratory barrack rooms were also a target for pranks because of their attitude, and breaking the unwritten laws that every barrack room or mess has. One lad always got back in the barrack room after a night out in the NAAFI or in town a little the worse for wear and said a loud 'Hello' to all who were sleeping or trying to sleep and kick their beds, except Dick and me who were NCOs.

One night we decided to get our own back. We dismantled his bed and tied the parts to the barrack room rafters. We then moved all the beds, so that there was no apparent space for another bed. He came in as expected and said hello loudly and kicked the foot of several beds. When he got to the position where his bed should have been he saw a bed but someone was sleeping in it. Being a little inebriated and thinking he had made a mistake, he looked at the label that was at the foot of all the beds and saw that it was not his. He went all down the line. His name was not on any of the beds. We heard a quiet 'Hmmm' and a quiet exit from the barrack room. We heard doors opening and closing from other parts of the barrack block. After ten to fifteen minutes he came back quietly. We were peeping just over the bedclothes. He came to my bed space and slowly looked again at my label. Obviously he was in the right room. Why he had not realised this before when he looked at the labels I can only put it down to his inebriated state.

Then loudly he said, 'What the fuck's going on here?' He switched on the lights.

'Turn the bloody lights off!' shouted Dick, 'And that's an order.'

'Where's my bloody bed?' Looking around and seeing smiling faces and eyes looking up at the ceiling, he followed their gaze up to the rafters. 'You bastards' he mumbled.

'I hope you're not directing that comment at me soldier' I said.

'Er, no corp' he mumbled. 'Someone give me a hand please?'

'Piss off' said Dick.

After a couple of minutes he pulled the barrack room table under the hanging bed and with lots of noise and swearing got his bed down and managed to assemble it. The bolting together took quite some time. He got the message however, because from then on he came in quietly and got into his 'pit' without disturbing anyone.

One day I examined a culture plate from a case of tonsillitis. It had beta haemolytic streptococci, the main cause of tonsillitis. Whilst writing the results on the form I scratched myself with the point of my pencil. The following day I felt a little feverish and my thumb was a little sore, but I thought I was coming down with a cold, so I did not take too much notice. Unfortunately, or perhaps fortunately as it turned out, I was on fire picket duty the following day. I had to sleep in at the BMH. We not only had our laboratory duties but we also had to do hospital duties.

I had to check the corridors and cellars throughout the hospital. It was quite a long walk checking locks on doors. A torch was needed in the basement cellars as lights had to be switched off. This duty done I was feeling a little under the weather, sweating profusely and somewhat light headed. I proceeded quickly to the night duty room for a lie down. The other two soldiers who were on picket duty were checking fire extinguishers and the perimeter grounds and making sure lights were out in the camp.

I got into bed, still sweating profusely. After about fifteen minutes I began to shake. I was having a rigor and felt weak and dizzy. One of the soldiers on picket duty, also from the CPL, came in to say good night. 'Christ! You all right corporal?' he said.

'No' I said, 'Go and get a medical officer.'

He dashed out and shortly came back with the MO on duty. He quickly checked me over, finding swollen glands in my groin and axilla (armpit).

'Get this man to the wards!' he shouted. Two nursing orderlies came in and lifted me out of the bed and slowly walked me to one of the wards. If they had not been supporting me I would have buckled. I was put to bed with my jacket slung over the metal headrest. The MO spoke to one of the QARANC nurses. 'Give him a million units of penicillin now.' I was turned over and penicillin injected into my buttock. Blood was also taken for culture, white cell count and my haemoglobin.

I was bathed frequently and given plenty to drink by the QARANCs, but knew little about it. The blood culture turned out to be positive for beta haemolytic streptococci and my white cell count was very high.

I slept fitfully, but my rigors had stopped by the morning. I was still feverish and weak. I was well looked after with more jabs in my buttocks. Thank God for penicillin. It had only started to be used towards the end of WWII. Sulphonamides would probably not have helped much. I probably wouldn't have made it without an antibiotic.

That week I became friendly with a Royal Air Force national serviceman. He, like myself, was in a single room, directly opposite mine. He was recovering from salmonella food poisoning. We got together and played board games for hours. We soon got tired of this and after the matron's inspection, the matron being a colonel in the QARANCs, we got dressed. This consisted of our uniforms, except we had to wear white shirts and a red tie. This was regular issue to make patients stand out. We were on the first floor, so we had to use the fire escape to get out. The NAAFI fortunately was just across the road. I knew the staff there and the clientele and would not have had too much of a problem, but to be on the safe side I took the RAF chap to the corporals' mess. We both got back before the next inspection and the visit with the medicine trolley.

One morning we were told that we were to be inspected by an RAMC colonel, a surgeon accompanied by matron and the usual retinue of officers and the BMH CO. We had to stand outside our rooms and then step aside when the colonel wanted to look inside the room. As per the barrack room the blankets etc had to be boxed and everything tidy with plenty of bull, helped by the QARANC nurses and RAMC nursing orderlies.

This inspection did not worry the RAF man. He knelt in front of his doorway with his knees in his shoes so he looked like a dwarf. When the column of officers came to his room he clicked his knees together and saluted. Eyebrows were raised but no words spoken. Then the colonel laughed, realising what was up, and said 'I made a good job of you lad. On your feet now.' The RAF chap went up a notch in my estimation of him.

The only other time I had to go on sick parade, so to speak, was when I was pushing a length of rubber tubing onto a glass tube whilst preparing transfusion blood-taking kits. The rubber was dipped in chloroform to make it slippery and easier to slide onto the glass. There was obviously insufficient chloroform on the rubber and the glass tube was invisibly fractured. As I pushed, the glass shattered and the jagged end went through my right hand between thumb and forefinger. The other end stuck out about two inches. There was not much blood but one of my staff saw it and said 'I'll go and fetch the captain'. This he did and the captain looked at it and twisted the glass and pulled. Nothing happened. He then escorted me to the BMH casualty department with the glass tubing sticking out of my hand like an arrow. The casualty department managed to get it free, not without some pain. It then began to bleed profusely. I then went to the X-ray dept. Fortunately the wound was free of glass. I was stitched up and bandaged. My hand looked like it had a boxing glove on.

Incidentally sick parades always puzzled me. If you were sick you had to go on a special parade with your washing-up gear, mug and pyjamas. You were inspected and marched off to the MO on duty. To me, if you managed this ordeal you were not that sick. However most of the time it was for feet. Those with athlete's foot would be excused boots and sometimes parades. They wore ordinary shoes as long as they were black.

Two days after my accident Dick and I went off to town for a meal and a drink. At the Altes Gasthaus Leve we ordered our meal, and when it arrived I had difficulty cutting my Wiener schnitzel with my bandaged hand. A waitress, seeing this, immediately came over, shooed me up along the bench seat, sat down beside me and cut up my meat. 'Danke schön' I said. 'Bitte' she replied, and sticking a fork in a piece of cut meat she proceeded to feed me. This, nice as it was and comical to Dick, was a little too much. I gracefully declined. This was the first time I had considered the difference between continental waiter/ waitress service and the English service. On the continent it was a respected career and not a job on a servant level as it was in England.

Our captain I/C (in charge) CPL was on duty at the BMH one evening. As I have mentioned we all had to do some duties for the BMH apart from our pathology duties. Before he went on duty he asked the CPL NCOs to see him in his office at 1700 hours.

'I have seen the QMS' (Quarter Master Sergeant) he said, 'and I would like volunteers to help throughout the night as we have a nursing orderly who has, to put it bluntly, flipped. This morning he went berserk and smashed up one of the wards and tipped two patients out of their beds. At the moment he is sedated but still violent. Can you all do an extra duty two hours on and two hours off throughout the night?'

'Yes' we replied.

'Pick two others and report to me at 1800 hours then, OK?'

'Yes sir' we answered. 'You'll get time off to compensate and I'll buy you all a drink at the NAAFI.' 'That will do nicely,' I said.

We reported for duty at 1800 hours. Dick picked Tony to be with him and I picked Taffy. I was on first shift. One of the QARANC nurses showed us the room and told us to give her a shout if there was a problem. The bed was occupied by a little fellow about five feet tall whom I recognised as one of the orderlies who did general duties like shovelling coal for the boilers and general cleaning chores. He obviously had not passed any of his nursing qualifications. One side of the iron bed was up and the other was against the wall to prevent him falling out. They had also tied him by the wrists with tape to the bed in case he started thrashing about. I also remembered him in the camp swimming pool. Actually it was the large water tank used in case of fire and in the summer everyone, it seemed, swam in it. We used to spend a lot of the time swimming under water to get away from the biting horse flies which had a saw-like proboscis to saw at the skin and then suck up the blood and serum produced. They were very numerous and their bite was extremely painful. He was often in the 'pool'. I can remember him diving in from the side and swimming the lengths back and forth mostly under water. The tank was about twenty yards long. I thought at first he was getting away from the horse flies, but he did not come up for air until he had swum two lengths. This he did regularly.

He was very quiet in the bed for about ten minutes and then he started moaning and waving his arms about. He started to look around the room and shake the sides of his bed. He looked at Taffy and me for a long time. He then dived under the bedclothes and started 'swimming'. We restrained him from thrashing about and he went to sleep. After two hours the other team relieved us. We went to the NAAFI for our two-hour break. At the turn around apparently nothing happened.

This continued until 0100 hours when the other team called us back because he was trying to climb out of the bed and through the window at the head of the bed. He started to shout, fight and scream. Two QARANC nurses came in to help. I told one of the team to get the captain. The QARANC went and came back shortly with our captain armed with syringe etc to sedate him. We lowered the side of the bed and he immediately tried to make a getaway. With three men holding him down with difficulty and the nurses holding his arm ready for the injection he started to fight and kept jerking his arm. For his size he was extremely strong. I took the place of one of the QARANC nurses and grabbed his arm in a lock. He threw me and the others holding him to one side and with a leap stood up in bed and removed his pyjamas and threw them out of the bed.

We jumped him and held him down. I had his arm in a lock again and the captain had his syringe ready. 'Oh my God!' exclaimed one of the nurses. 'What's up?' said Dick. I turned and saw that the nurse was looking at the patient's naked body.

I have never seen anything like it, even on a big man. He did not have an erection but his flaccid penis was nine to ten inches long and three inches wide. The captain looked at me, covered the patient with a sheet and said 'Ready?' 'Yes sir' I replied and held down on the arm tightly. He got the needle into the vein without any bother but keeping it in with the patient writhing and screaming was not easy. After two minutes he relaxed so we relaxed our hold. He leapt up into a sitting position, swinging his arms about, and then collapsed. We were all sweating but relieved.

The captain thanked us and dismissed the nurses, who left smiling broadly. The following day about midday he was transported to BMH Hanover, a mental hospital. That was the last we heard. The captain was as good as his word and thanked us with beers all round that evening.

That August a new member arrived at CPL nicknamed 'Baggers'. His first name was John. He was a paramedic and qualified in biochemistry. He wore his parachute with wings on his BD and sported a moustache like Dick, but jet black. He did not wax it like Dick, who only did it for spite towards the RSM whose moustache was not as big. On parades Dick was usually told to get his boots cleaned or get a haircut by the RSM.

Baggers had a mouthful of white, even teeth and seemed always to be smiling. He was very noticeable, especially to the QARANC nurses. He was posted to my crystalloid dept, and arrived about the same time as our colonel left to go back to Millbank Royal Army Medical College. A week earlier the colonel had called me into his office. 'Corporal, would you examine this ZN?' (Zeil Neilson stain for TB slide examination – mycobacterium tuberculosis bacilli show up red against a methylene blue stained background under the microscope known as acid fast bacilli). 'I want a second opinion' said the colonel. I looked down the microscope and was a little puzzled as to why he wanted a second opinion. The slide of sputum was packed with TB bacilli.

'Well?' said the colonel.

'A good positive sir,' I replied.

'Yes' he said quietly, 'it is my sputum'.

He was flown back to Millbank for treatment.

Another bit of excitement in a different way was a specimen of Admiral Doenitz's prostate sent to us for histological section to examine for any malignancy. Of course all the staff wanted a microscope slide stained with haematoxylin and eosin to keep for themselves. Mine unfortunately got broken along with other glassware such as beakers with the eagle and swastika engraved on them during customs check, when an officer emptied my kit bag on the floor during my leave. Normally they were not that bothered about checking, but some foolish cook was smuggling tins of corned beef in his kit bag. How he managed to lift it I have no idea, nor do I understand why he wanted corned beef so badly.

Our new colonel was keen on rugby football. He was pleased to learn that members of the CPL staff were in the BMH Münster team. He encouraged us by giving us as much time off for training and playing as possible. He was also keen on cricket, so Dick and I took advantage of this too.

Dick and I were also in the tennis championship pairs, so on Wednesdays instead of remaining in our 'pits' we would be either playing rugby, cricket or tennis. Baggers was also in the cricket team. Both our Welsh members of staff and another Scot were in the rugby team.

'Baggers' was qualified in histology and morbid anatomy. He introduced us to home-made gin and tonic. The histology dept. had to preserve specimens in formaldehyde but had to stain the slides with the aid of 100% ethyl alcohol. Not meths, which is methyl alcohol and very detrimental to one's visual health, hence getting 'blind' drunk. When diluted with two parts water and a few crystals of citric acid added it made a very passable G&T. However we had to be careful, as about every three months inspectors would pay us a visit to examine the register listing the amount used and when. It always seemed to happen that about this time there was an accident whereby certain parts of the register were burnt.

Our barrack rooms were inspected every Wednesday morning after parade so that the afternoons were free for sporting activities or a lie in. We therefore had to 'bull' our whole barrack room and have our beds and kit laid out in the usual manner, but with less bull than during our first three months' training. Our floors were polished with a reddish army issue polish which was flicked onto the floor and then, using an old blanket wrapped around a soldier, it was pulled up and down the room until it shone. The passenger did not like it very much when we did the corners, as we swung him hard against the walls. I mention this because we had to do major repairs to our polished floor when one of the lads accidentally dropped some of his home-made G&T on the floor. It took all the thick polish off and took hours to build it back up and polish it to a good shine again. 'Christ, what's it doing to our guts then?' said Baggers.

Wooden barrack room tables had to be scrubbed. We had the only barrack room that had a polished table. When I took over the barrack room the table had a very deep burn in the shape of an iron. Someone from the previous intake of soldiers must have left the iron flat down on the table whilst doing his ironing. Polishing it disguised it quite well and it was not noticed for a long time. It came to be noticed however when Brian (another one) was ironing his trousers on the table. I had strictly forbidden this. Ironing was to be done in the washroom. Ironing his second-best BD trousers on the table left a deep red stripe along the crease. We were due for a second-best BD parade and inspection that same morning. If your BD or boots were in a state of disrepair, then they would be replaced.

During the inspection the CO walking down the line ahead of the RSM noticed the red stripe down Brian's trousers. 'What is that soldier?'

'Polish sir' said Brian.

The RSM shouted at him, 'Why didn't you iron on the table? Why on the floor laddie?'

'I did iron on the table sir' Brian replied.

'There are no polished tables for other ranks. Whose barrack room are you in?'

'Corporal Eldridge's sir.'

I came to attention, calling Brian all the insulting names I could think of under my breath and stepped one pace forward. 'Sir' I said and explained the reason for our polished table. The CO said he would take a look after the inspection. We marched back to our barrack rooms and shortly after we were visited by the CO and the RSM. The CO went straight to the table. 'All right sergeant major we will allow this, but try and get a replacement sometime. It does after all cover the burn.' We never received a replacement but were happy in the knowledge that we were the only other rank barrack room in the RAMC to have a polished table.

Our crystalloid department provided transfusion equipment, citrate bottles and glucose bottles for blood collection and bottles of sterile saline supplying all the BMHs in Germany. We kept quite a large stock but sometimes there was quite a run on bottles for saline drips. When the order came we packed them in wooden crates and drove them to the railway station in the CPL army Humber truck. This we quite enjoyed. The trip to the station usually took longer than necessary as a beer in a Gasthaus on the way back was always on the cards, to the delight of our German driver, Klaus, who did most of the lifting too.

We took longer than usual on one trip. A German civilian ambulance that we were following on the way back to the BMH braked suddenly and we hit it in the rear, smashing the back doors in and shunting the stretcher against the driver's cabin. The German police arrived quickly on the scene but so did our military police, who quickly shooed the German police away. They quickly sorted it out, asking me what speed we were doing etc, and sent us on our way. Fortunately there were no patients in the ambulance. This was still the period of military occupational law.

Two months later when the German government took the reins again, the situation just described would have been very different. In fact the attitude of the German public towards us changed. They were no longer quite so friendly, or perhaps I should say tolerant.

I had put up on the wall a long chart for the whole year in the form of a graph showing how much stock of the various bottles we held. Underneath below the days and months the lads also drew cartoons and made comments about all our exploits as a record. During an inspection our colonel thought it was a great idea, but the cartoons and comments had to go. This was disappointing and spoilt our fun. If the army liked an idea it had to be made part of their 'bull' regime, so sometimes it is better not to try and improve the system.

The colonel told us that when we reached a thousand bottles in stock he would fund a party for us. This was unbelievable, what a nice guy. I made things more efficient by setting up our own Benedicts test area for glucose estimation instead of sending samples of our glucose bottles to the biochemistry dept. This again became part of the system.

It took one and a half months to reach the total of a thousand bottles in stock because every time we neared our target there was an order from a BMH for us to deliver a consignment of various transfusion bottles and sets.

Finally I reported to the colonel that we had reached our target. He wondered if all the bottles had been inspected properly for any foreign bodies in solutions. The bottles were held up to a light against a black background and dust etc could be spotted easily.

'Of course sir,' I said.

'Hmm I did not expect you to reach that target so soon,' mumbled the colonel. This surprised me. We should have hit the target earlier but for the outgoing orders. 'Very well corporal, buy your booze and get the kitchen staff to provide sandwiches and I suggest you invite some QARANC nurses. The captain has a record player I believe. Send me the bill, will you?' I couldn't believe it.

We decided to have the party that Wednesday in the laboratory corridor. We set up tables and loaded them with sandwiches from the cookhouse. Of course the sergeant in the Catering Corps responsible had to be invited along with his corporal, who we knew well. He was our rugby wing three-quarter. Crates of beer were bought from the NAAFI with a few bottles of wine for the nurses. Six were able to come. The record player was fine. The Captain only had Bach, Holst and Tchaikovsky, but he managed to borrow Sinatra, Crosby and Ella Fitzgerald from another officer. One of our other officers, a major from Malta, supplied us with more records. We showed our gratitude but only played his collection of Vera Lynn songs once. The colonel did not bat an eyelid at the cost and also supplied two bottles of whisky.

The party was a success. The nurses enjoyed the dancing with many partners.

A thirteen- stone nurse called, Anne had a little too much wine and did rather a lot of dancing. The other nurses spent most of their time drinking with Dick and Baggers, sitting on their laps. Also invited were our two male German staff along with our young cleaner who brought her husband along. She added to the food with several bowls of Kartoffelsalat (potato salad).

Anne insisted that I have a dance with her as it was a jazz number. At the end of a twirl she missed my hand and sat down heavily on a chair along the corridor. The four legs of the chair went outwards in different directions with a crash. This caused an uproarious bout of laughing, but not from Q. He said 'Brian, tomorrow the chair will have to be repaired in time for inspection. I will supply the wood glue and you will repair it, right?'

'Yes Q,' I replied unhappily.

The nurses had to be back by 2300 hours, but the rest of us were determined to finish the booze. Dick helped it along quite well, especially with the scotch, being an Edinburgh lad. The corridors were wet with spilt beer. Dick wanted to offer our captain a glass of scotch but slipped on the wet floor on his way over to him, banging his head on the corner of a table. He was out for the count, partly due to the alcohol I think. The captain said he would be all right once he had a sleep, so we were to take him back to his bed. A door was taken off its hinges and Dick placed upon it. We lifted it onto our shoulders and marched back to the barrack room in slow time funeral fashion, to the delight of some soldiers as we passed the cookhouse.

He was a little better in the morning, albeit with a nasty headache and a bruise and a bit tottery. Taffy was also the worse for wear. Unfortunately we were due for our morning parade. We managed to get there on time, but George and I had to prop Dick up between us while Baggers and Moose surreptitiously held up Taffy. When the RSM came along the line we had to leave them without us as props. They swayed a little but managed with concentration to keep upright. Unfortunately Dick with his moustache, the one that was now better than the RSM's, had not shaved, and this was immediately spotted.

'Did you shave this morning corporal?' asked the RSM quietly.

'Yes sir' answered Dick, 'But my razor was blunt and I did not have time to go to the NAAFI and get more blades.'

'You could have gone last night before your party laddie.' The RSM shouted with glee. 'Two days, CB. I'll see your colonel. OK?'

'Yes sir' mumbled Dick.

It so happened he was on duty that night and I was on the following night. We swapped, because I was sure he would sleep through the night. I didn't feel too bad.

I repaired the chair as ordered but did not expect it to stand anyone even a little heavier than average. The QARANC nurse, Anne, was involved in another incident on Corps Day that I will never forget.

Corps Day is on the 23rd June and is to celebrate the Royal Warrant of 1898. The title 'The Medical Staff Corps' was changed to the RAMC by Queen Victoria. Corps Day started off with a serious inspection, so there was plenty of bull in the barrack rooms. One of the lads in our room however was given two days' CB. His clothes laid out on the bed were in good order and in their right places. His blankets were properly boxed, but his socks were at fault. They were properly squared around a square of cardboard. However when the CO lifted them up with his stick, one was just the top of the sock wrapped around the cardboard and the other sock practically fell apart. The woolly rag surrounding numerous holes hanging from the swagger stick was a sight to behold, and we had great difficulty keeping a straight face.

I was corporal on duty I/C reception that evening. There was to be a Corps Dance, and I was responsible for security. The morning was taken up with the obligatory church parade. We marched in best BD, everything highly bulled along the road and watched by the German public. Their interest was not in us in particular but in part of a Scots regiment playing bagpipes ahead of us. I could march all day to the sound of the pipes. It was very stirring.

The dance was attended by all those not on duty, including the officers. The regulars wore their dress uniforms, not the usual khaki but dark blue with a red stripe down the trouser. The dance went off well. Invitations to other regiments and corps in the Münster area were also sent. We had WRACs (Women's Royal Army Corp), WAAFs, (Women's Auxiliary Air Force) and our QARANC nurses for dancing partners. There was plenty of beer and spirits being drunk and the Münster BMH band were playing at the end of the dining hall. All the chairs and tables were placed around the perimeter. There were a few hundred people present.

We had many spot prize dances and one where the dancers had to cross a 'river' indicated by two chalked lines about twenty feet apart down the middle of the hall. No one was allowed to dance in the 'river' but when the music stopped the man had to pick up his partner and cross it before the music started again. Of course there was a lot of bumping as dancers either side of the 'river' collided. Anyone caught in it when the music started was eliminated.

I was dancing with Anne, the QARANC nurse who broke the laboratory chair. I was fit and able to carry her thirteen stone across the 'river' without any problem, to the amusement of the crowd. I managed it seven times. However I was getting tired and with only ten couples left dancing, the music stopped. I lifted Anne up into my arms and charged across the 'river', but when we bumped into another couple I slipped and dropped her. She hit the floor with a crash on her ample backside with me on top of her. I put my hands out to break my fall and my right hand slid up her skirt, which had risen up past her knees.

All during the dance photographers were about taking various shots of the proceedings. I did not take much notice and was concerned whether Anne was all right and got her to her feet. She was none the worse for wear and we had a drink and a good laugh about the dance. The following morning however, the photographs were pinned on the dining room walls. My photo had been enlarged and I could see to my embarrassment and probably Anne's, when she saw it, that the photographer had taken the shot at the split second my hand had accidentally gone up her skirt with her ample legs akimbo. Anne however thought it was a great laugh when she saw it, so I felt a lot better. The rest of the BMH had great enjoyment out of it for some time after at my expense.

Towards the end of the dance an RASC lance corporal, a lorry driver for the BMH, got rather drunk. KRRC soldiers, also known as riflemen, who were at the dance were also quite drunk and had a reputation for fighting, but were no trouble at all. This lance corporal however must have seen me with Anne on the dance floor during the 'river' dance. He was making a nuisance of himself dancing with the nurses and WRAC's, trying to kiss them and putting his hand up their skirts. Dick, who was my second in command on duty for the evening had a complaint from one of the nurses. He pointed out the culprit, so I went up to him and cautioned him that the next complaint meant he would be out on his ear.

'Ain't doing nuffink corp' he said.

'Well, you've been warned,' I said.

I kept an eye on him and five minutes later he was at it again. I called Dick over and we hauled him off the dance floor and showed him the door. He did not want to go. I shoved him out and closed the door after telling him that if he came back again I would put him on a charge. As we turned and started back towards the dance hall the doors banged open and back in came the lance corporal. I turned and quickly ducked as a punch came swinging towards me. Dick was immediately behind me and the punch caught him on the forehead. Dick grabbed him, got him in a half-nelson and threw him out again.

The lance corporal was determined. He came back in again, but this time he was swinging a piece of wooden fencing from the perimeter gardens around the mess hall. It was about four feet long by three inches wide and flat. He took a swing at me, but I blocked it with my arm. My thick BD sleeve softened the blow a little. He swung again but being somewhat drunk was a little slow. I hit him in the face. He staggered and came at me again, kicking me in the shin as the piece of wood missed my shoulder. I went down. He was about to swing at me again with the fencing when Dick disarmed him and threw him to the ground with a judo hip throw. I thought then that he had had enough, so we left him on the ground.

Then the sound of footsteps behind us made me turn around quickly. He was at us again shouting and swearing. He did not have the piece of wood but carried instead a knife. It was one of those boy scout's knives that had a pebbled black handle and a spike for supposedly getting stones out of horse's hooves. This was closed, but the large blade was out. Since the episode during my marine engineering days, I do not like being threatened with a knife. I just went cold. I had lost my temper. I kicked him in the kneecap and punched him. He staggered back and came up against the wall of the boiler house by the kitchen attached to the mess hall. He dropped the knife. I hit him again and again and again, very systematically. His mouth was bleeding profusely. My knuckles were all skinned and he had teeth missing.

Fortunately Dick pulled me off. We got him to the BMH reception and into hospital, telling the duty MO that he was drunk and had fallen on a large perimeter stone. I did not of course charge him. I found out that he had lost six teeth from the top set. It is still very much on my conscience and I feel guilty for doing this cold-bloodedly to another person, no matter how much he deserved it. I have since come across others who did deserve such justice, and these types are on the increase. Perhaps it is lack of discipline and lack of values.

Dick and I cleaned up and went back to the dance, which was going very well. Only one of the corporals in the Army Catering Corp was aware of the incident. He looked at us and said 'He was trouble last year. He was a sergeant then. All under control?'

'Just about.' I replied.

'Come on' he said, 'I'll buy you both a drink'.

We had a huge glass of brandy each, probably used for cooking but nevertheless it was very acceptable. The corporal was billeted in the same block as me, but not the same barrack room. All the cooks were in the same room and we got on well with them. This is wise if you want to eat well.

Our rugby team was not very successful, mainly due to not having enough members off duty to play and other teams having men that were much bigger and better. We did however manage to get to the quarter-finals because of a bye, and had a nice trip to look forward to. It was to be staged at the rugby grounds in Iserlohn.

The rugby match before this was as usual a bit rough. We played in all weathers. Sometimes the pitch was so muddy that you couldn't distinguish who was on your side and who was the enemy. Our jerseys were red, which was handy as it did not show the blood. After a few tackles the ears got bunged up with mud and any call went literally on deaf ears. I often wondered how such big blokes in the tank regiment teams could get into the tanks. The KRRC riflemen were roughest. I was pleased we never had to play against the Marines or the Parachute regiments.

The weather was wet and the pitch very muddy, a quagmire. It was from the scrum that the ball was squeezed out and was half buried in the mud. It was more like the Eton Wall Game. The scrum half fell to his knees and did not pass the ball to me but just handed it over. I started to run with it. I was only about twenty yards from the try line. Every step became more difficult as I got taller with the mud sticking to the bottom of my boots. I turned to see if I had any back up, but all I could see was three large KRRC backs chasing after me. I assumed that's what they were as I couldn't see any red on their jerseys. It was like being in a dream where you try to run away from something but no matter how fast you try you do not make any progress and can't get away. I could hear their breathing and the sucking noise of their boots being pulled from the mud with effort. They were slowly gaining on me and I could not reach the line. It all seemed to be in slow motion, which I suppose it was. Five yards from the line I stopped and started to laugh, then turned to see the chasing trio sitting in the mud, also laughing. The game was abandoned.

We travelled to Iserlohn in a truck for the quarter-finals, which were incidentally Sevens. We arrived and parked amidst many tents and marquees. The marquees were for the officers and the tents for the other ranks, where we could get tea and sandwiches. The officers had beer and wine from their marquees. So even as a team there was still separation as to rank. However our officers came out of their marquee with crates of beer for us. Our first match was against a Hussars team, the same regiment as the soldier I had to escort to the Hook of Holland from Harwich.

We lost by just one try. We were not really fit enough for Sevens. It was exhausting. After the match we washed and changed, had more beers and enjoyed the rest of the day by watching the other matches. It was obvious that some players were quality. Some had played for the Harlequins and the Wasps, so we had no chance. Our best player was an Irish surgeon who played wing three quarter for one of the Irish teams. The rest of us were just school and local club players. I am still obsessed with the game.

The end of November was very wet and stormy, with storms

the like of which I had never seen before. One storm was really vicious. I was in the NAAFI playing snooker with Dick. There was thunder and lightning and rain coming down like stair rods. A lightning bolt hit the perimeter fence. The thunderous boom was instantaneous and the lightning travelled right around the camp along the fence, burning the wire and cracking some of the concrete posts. I think it was the shock wave that threw us on the floor, although some I think instinctively ducked. The air tingled and the hairs on my arms and at the back of my neck were as if I had goose pimples. There was a strange buzzing sound and a bluish glow in the corners of the room, possibly because of some metal there, but it seemed harmless. I enjoy thunderstorms because of their beauty, but I am still nervous of them nevertheless.

Three weeks later three members of the CPL were on ambulance duty together, me included. Another chore we had to contend with on top of our laboratory duties. Our colonel accepted it because he considered it an essential experience in our soldiering career.

The officers and sergeants were often trying to convince national servicemen that the RAMC was a good career. I must admit I was tempted. I could have signed on for another year to become a regular. Some did so at the very start. They received extra pay and it was a quicker route to promotion. I was fortunate in getting my stripes after only a month or so in Germany. Even Moose tried to persuade us to join the Canadian Medical Corps after our service. To join the Canadians would have given us a good pension, and our two years with the RAMC would be counted. One of the drawbacks was that we would have to be demobbed in Vancouver or somewhere in Canada. But it was worth a thought.

We chatted to the fire picket squad most of the evening and

played cards. They did their tour of the hospital compound and checked all the fire appliances. The reception staff on duty checked the barrack rooms and ordered lights out, and those that had passes to go into town were all back and accounted for.

At about midnight the reception duty officer got a call that there was some trouble in town and some soldiers had been injured. The RASC driver was called and we three jumped into the ambulance. After a bumpy twenty-minute ride we reached our given destination on the outskirts of town. It was not very peaceful. There was a lot of shouting as we piled out of the ambulance. We saw four soldiers. One was KRRC, one was tanks. The other two we found out were soldiers but were in civvies. The tank regiment soldier was up against a wall swinging and ducking as he was being attacked by two German youths. The KRRC chap was wrestling with another. One of the soldiers in civvies was bending over the other trying to revive him. The Gasthaus behind them from which we assumed they had been kicked out was closed.

As we pulled out the stretcher canvas from the back of the ambulance there was a lot of German shouting. I do not know what was being said and I continued to remove one of the stretcher poles and slide it through the canvas. Dick was bringing out the other pole. Two more youths joined the others who were laying into the tank regiment soldier. Dick saw this and instead of pushing the pole through the canvas he started swinging it at the German boys. Three backed off, but one was not quick enough and received a blow across his back, giving the soldier the opportunity to uppercut him and run towards the ambulance. Then it all went quiet. Everyone had disappeared apart from the soldiers.

I questioned the tank regiment man regarding the soldier lying unconscious on the ground. No one seemed to know. His nose was bleeding but that seemed to be the only damage. 'Where is he from?' I asked. 'Welsh Borderers I think,' said the KRRC man. 'Right, then let's get him back to the hospital. Is everyone else OK?' I asked. 'Yeah' came the reply. 'And can you drop us off at the KRRC barracks? But first, this lad to the BMH.'

There was no need to give the others a lift because at that moment the MPs arrived. Ian explained the situation to them and with smiles and jokes we left them.

On the journey back we were a little concerned. After loosening the soldier's clothing there seemed to be no movement from him and he did not seem to be breathing. We lifted his eyelids and there did not seem to be much sign of life. I put a mirror to his mouth but there was no mist on the glass. We cleared his nose of blood, laid him on his side and checked his airways. 'I think he's dead,' whispered Ian, another Scot.

We started artificial respiration, but almost immediately we were at the BMH. We got him to the casualty department, where he was given oxygen. He sat up immediately, babbling away incoherently. After being examined by the MO on duty it was decided he was dead drunk. He started to vomit and was given some coffee. He seemed to have recovered somewhat, but was still babbling incoherently.

'I know what it is' said Ian, 'It's bloody Welsh.'

'Are you sure?' I asked.

'I think so, he's so drunk he's forgotten his English.'

I sent Ian back to the barrack room to get Taffy out of his pit to help us. I thought he spoke some Welsh – at least he sang rugby songs in Welsh. Taffy arrived, not particularly pleased to be got out of bed. However he spoke to the drunken soldier in Welsh. There was an immediate response. He put his arms around Taffy and grinned. Taffy grimaced from the smell of beer and vomit.

'Ask where he's from, Taffy,' I said. Apparently he was a Welsh Borderer from I think Blenheim Barracks. We telephoned them and they sent transport. He would be put on a charge for being out after curfew and would also get extra punishment for being drunk and disorderly.

We finished the rest of duty without incident.

Chapter 10

Winding down towards demob

That month, instead of going back to 'Blighty' for my two weeks' leave I used one week to travel down the Rhine and the Mosel with George. We did not have very much money, so we decided to catch a train to Cologne (Köln) and do some walking. We used our army backpacks for our gear, towels, clean underwear and washing kit. We decided to try to reach Cochem. We did not intend to walk all the way of course, but to catch the occasional train and make use of Fremdenzimmers for bed and breakfast because they were pretty cheap.

We travelled to Cologne, walked around and then caught a train to Bonn and then another train to Andernach and then to Koblenz. We decided then to walk to Cochem, and then perhaps to Bernkastel on the Mosel. It took longer than we envisaged.

It was dark – very dark. We had a torch, but there was nothing on the road, no lights from any houses and no moon. After about an hour of stumbling in the dark along a road irregularly pitted with potholes, I saw lights some way off. 'Ah' said George, 'Thank Christ. Signs of habitation.'

After a couple of minutes we seemed to be almost on top of them, and just then they went out. We stopped, puzzled. They were glow-worms. We walked for another half an hour, until at about ten o'clock we saw lit up a sort of castle in the air and made our way towards it. Before reaching it however we stumbled across a small hamlet of about four houses by the river. We had left the Rhine and were on the banks of the Mosel. None offered any accommodation. We were tired and hungry and thirsty. After a while we found a bar by the river, but no sleeping accommodation. At least we had something to eat and drink, beer and sausages.

We decided that our only alternative was to kip by the river. It was quiet and the only sound was from the river. We dumped our gear on the grass bank under a tree and laid our towels out under it. We put on extra clothes because it was pretty chilly and used our backpacks as pillows. We were tired but we did not sleep well. The ground was very uncomfortable and the mist, coming up from the river, made it very damp, particularly our towels.

In the morning we got up and I decided to go down to the river and have a wash, a shave and clean my teeth. I gathered my washing kit and grabbed my towel from the grass. The grass was pink – it was a carpet of worms. George's patch was the same. The heat from our bodies must have brought them to the surface. We shook our towels, not that they would be much use to dry us but at least it removed the worms.

After our ablutions, feeling relatively refreshed, we went back to the bar by the river for breakfast and to use their toilets. We then took photos of the bridges and the river. It was very picturesque. We sat on a bench, had a smoke and decided to walk back to the station and catch the train to Koblenz.

After a few miles I realised I had left my camera on the bench by the river. 'Oh shit!' I shouted. I was in two minds whether to leave it or not. George said, 'Come on we'll both go back.' I found it still on the bench, so we decided to spend the day there by the river. We enjoyed ourselves sitting outside the bar drinking beer and eating our sausages.

We found a small Gasthaus with a vacant room, although it used up most of the money we had left. At breakfast we only had coffee, explaining to the landlady our financial plight. She nevertheless gave us bread and cereals and jam on the house. I found some Germans, especially in the country, were very hospitable.

I was now beginning to think about demob. I was due for it in February 1956, so that left me about seven months to do. It was still a little way off but I could see the light at the end of the tunnel. Soldiers who only had a couple of weeks before their demob usually started to enjoy themselves and were classified as demob-happy bastards. I was looking forward to it in some respects, but I knew I would miss many of my fellow soldiers. Some I felt were as close to me as my brother. This sort of comradeship in the forces is very strong.

Most of the CPL staff became close. I say most, as some just did not get along. A lance corporal and another member of the laboratory staff could not stand each other although they were in the same barrack room and both in the haematology department. Dick, who was I/C haematology, mentioned it to me.

One evening after work a row started in the barrack room. The lance corporal who had been 'made up' just two weeks previously was getting on everyone's nerves as he was using his rank to order the other staff members around. A fledgling trying out his wings before flight, as it were. Dick and I both outranked him and we should have taken him aside and given him a quiet word of advice. He was also a 'bootlicker' or a 'brown tongue/arse licker', which was frowned upon. He never tried his 'bootlicking' with Dick or me. He knew he would fail, as Dick and I got on with practically all the staff including the officers.

There was lot of shouting and shoving. The lance corporal had apparently told Tony, the other lad, that he was not doing his cleaning duties properly when it was his turn on the roster. Apart from inspection days the rest of the week was very lax and we did not spend too much time and effort on tidiness. Cleanliness however was a different matter. But this was not the case with Tony. He was clean and tidy personally and in the barrack room. It was obviously a case of incompatibility. The lance corporal said 'I've bloody well had enough of you. You're bloody insubordinate and I don't like your fucking attitude when I tell you to do things.'

'All right, what are you going to do about it lance-fucking-corporal?' said Tony sarcastically. 'Right, that's it. We'll sort this out outside,' the lance corporal shouted.

'I'm off duty and I'm staying right here,' replied Tony.

'Right then, we'll settle it here' shouted the lance corporal loudly.

They were both about the same height and build except that Tony was a little slimmer. The lance corporal removed his BD blouse and rolled up his sleeves. Tony was already in shirt-sleeve order. They stood facing each other.

'How do you want it?' asked the lance corporal.

'However you like,' said Tony.

'OK you bastard, then it's all in' sneered the lance corporal. 'No holds barred?'

'OK' replied Tony and immediately kneed the lance corporal in the groin, bending him over. As he started to straighten Tony delivered an uppercut that dropped him on his back. He started to rise, but Tony delivered a left hook high on his right temple.

Dick then stepped in. 'That's enough Tony. Get off him.' Tony was astride his chest. 'I think that's settled that' I said.

The lance corporal was in a bad way. He was groggy and bleeding from the mouth and the orbit of the eye.

'I think you had better get to reception,' I said.

'Right' said Dick loudly, 'Fancy slipping on the floor and banging your head on the side of your bed, and sober too. Understand?'

'Yes' mumbled the lance corporal.

'Right come on then,' and Dick took him off to reception for medical treatment. He had an X-ray and had a week off duties. He had a small fracture of the right orbit of the eye.

There was no more trouble between the two, although they avoided each other as much as possible. When the lance corporal was discharged from the hospital I spoke to our captain regarding the antagonism between the two. He consequently moved the lance corporal to the histology department, and I moved him out of our barrack room into the other CPL barrack room. He did not like it, but he had no option.

On Tuesday nights we usually spent the evening in the NAAFI before getting down to bulling up the barrack room for Wednesday inspection. We usually made quite a noise and bulled until late, annoying the other barrack room, who had completed their bulling earlier and had gone to bed. They usually shouted at us to keep quiet, but this we ignored, singing even louder whilst polishing the floor.

They must have had enough one Tuesday, because when we awoke on the Wednesday our lovely bulled barrack room was completely changed. The whole floor and table were completely covered in cabbages. The boys from the other barrack room had pulled them up from a neighbouring farm. The farmland came right up to our perimeter fence.

We had to rush around like mad to get the room cleaned up and to get the cabbages back over the perimeter wire. Washing away the mud was the worst part, but we got the message.

Ray in the next barrack room was a bird fancier. He had a large folder containing birds' wings. I was a bit dubious about his love of birds. He was more of a collector.

He had bought a .22 bolt- action rifle in Germany and shot the birds, removing a wing and sticking it in a folder after preserving it in formaldehyde. He had them all neatly labelled and catalogued. Why he did not just observe them with binoculars I do not know.

One night after celebrating somebody's birthday in the corporals' mess we went to bed rather the worse for wear. In the morning I awoke nursing a hangover and got a fright. I thought I was hallucinating. I lifted my head gingerly from the pillow and saw perched on the rail at the foot of the bed a sparrowhawk. It scared me because I thought it was the drink. It was looking at me, eyes staring and its beak positively dangerous. Ray had not shot it but had found it during his bird forays in the woods with a broken wing. That morning he took it to the MO on duty and together they covered it with a blanket and then splinted and bandaged the wing. It was then taken into town to a vet, where it eventually recovered. It was not released back into the wild but given to the zoo. I really thought that morning that the booze had gotten to me at last.

I spent that Christmas in Germany. It was quite interesting in that on Christmas morning the Sergeant Major and his retinue of corporals came round all the barrack rooms and instead of the usual 'Hands off cocks and on socks' and the shaking of the bed we were given tea and rum in bed. Incidentally when on reception duty you never shook a soldier in bed to wake him up, he might in his sleepy state take a swing at you and if it connected it would be the only time he would get away with it. It was considered a sort of self -defence as the soldier was not completely aware on waking.

One of our corporals, a regular of twelve years, did not live in the camp but had a house with his German wife about ten minutes' walk from the BMH. It was still army accommodation but married quarters. Once a week a couple of us were invited to the house for drinks and an evening meal. We enjoyed this very much. His wife made a good Kartoffel salad, which we enjoyed so much that she had to make twice as much on our second visit and there was still none left over. This was a treat for us as the camp food was variable. Fridays was either fish or curry. Most soldiers chose the fish as the curry was always a fluorescent green colour and seemed to throb with heat. You needed gallons of water to cool down after eating it. You always expected your spoon to dissolve in it and I think pounds were lost in the sweat produced from our brows. There was always five gallons of curry in a pan left uneaten to be thrown away. The strength and colour never varied, even though the catering officer was told many times. Left-over food was sent to farms for the pigs. I felt sorry for the pigs.

After one visit to the corporal's home on my own I was walking back to the barracks through a small wood. It was very dark. I heard some rustling ahead of me. I stopped and listened; nothing. I cautiously approached the bushes where the rustling was coming from. There was more rustling and some movement of the branches. The guardroom gates of the BMH could be seen ahead of me down the path about two minutes away. I did not want whoever or whatever to jump out at me as I passed the bushes along the path. Perhaps it was a fox. I had heard that there were wolves, but I had never seen one and it was probably only a rumour.

I was a little frightened, so without another thought I charged at the bush yelling. As I broke through the bush I lashed out with my feet, branches whipping my arms and my face. My boot hit something solid and there was a grunt. I lashed out again and connected. There was an immediate shout. I carried on through the bush for a couple of yards and then stopped and turned around. I saw a Polish gatekeeper trying to pull up his trousers and still grunting. I had kicked him while he was having a crap. Polish workers manned the guardroom gate, while the guardroom and reception were manned by British personnel. Why this was so I never found out, or indeed enquired.

I quickly ran down the path and through the gate, reported to reception and then back to my barrack room. I heard nothing further about the incident, but it shook me, though not as much, I imagine, as the Polish gatekeeper.

I usually walked the woods with one or two others and only occasionally on my own. Walking through woods is quite a daunting experience at night, hearing the wildlife around you. It is wise, although difficult, when walking through a wood at night not to look back over your shoulder as it makes you more apprehensive than you are already. Why I do not know. I think the imagination takes hold. An ancient instinct. It is better to keep going, walking quickly and trying not to run, again very difficult.

After Christmas I was beginning to get demob happy. At the beginning of January I was called in to see the CO of the BMH and he asked me to sit down.

'You have done well here,' he said, 'and I have good reports from your officers. I would like you to consider signing on as a regular soldier.' He went on in some detail regarding the benefits of signing on for another year or more, but I was keen to go back to civvy street and carry on with my career there.

'I don't think so sir' I said. 'I already have a position waiting for me in the laboratories in the UK.'

'Well' he replied, 'think it over and if you change your mind come and see me. You realise that when you are demobbed you are still on Army Emergency Reserve for three years?'

This meant that if there was any crisis within three years of my demobilisation, I would be called back in.

Most demob happy soldiers prepare for a party a couple of weeks before they go. These thoughts for me were put to one side because a big exercise involving the whole of the BAOR, including the Canadian, French, Belgian and US armies was to take place. It was called 'Battle Royal'. The CPL was, apart from a skeleton staff, to be a field ambulance division for blood transfusion duties. The staff on duty had to obtain a pass stating that they were exempt on that day or week from these 'war games'.

Dick, Taffy, George, Alan and I were not on duty. We packed up the field laboratory equipment in crates and loaded them into our army Humber. We had to drive out of town to a field and set up a laboratory under a small tent. It was thick with snow and very cold. We wore our gloves and several layers of clothing under our greatcoats. We were part of blue section – red section was the enemy. We had to prepare ourselves by covering ourselves up with snow as camouflage to the best of our ability, although not very successfully. This was apparently to avoid capture by the 'Reds'. We had blue flashes on our steel helmets and shoulder flaps. Our driver was an RASC man, not our usual German civilian driver. He carried a rifle in the Humber cabin. There were others of the 'Blue' contingent from the BMH, nursing orderlies, QARANC nurses and an MO.

We dug in a few hundred yards from their hospital tents in a copse, hid the Humber as best we could and unpacked the laboratory equipment, using the boxes for seats and benches. We covered the tent and the Humber with snow. It was early morning. We had some food but were expected back at the BMH before 2200 hours, so we did not have to sleep out. At midday we ate our sandwiches provided by the cookhouse, brewed up some tea and settled down for a boring day.

About 1400 hours we heard and saw a commotion over the other side of the field. Soldiers were running across the field and rounding up some of the BMH personnel. They had red flashes. They did not take any notice of us. We were difficult to see as we were covered in snow. I told everyone to move away and dig in in the snow away from our encampment and away round the other side of the copse.

After lying low for about half an hour, we heard a dog barking. It was a large black and white Labrador type with a collar, and it came towards us wagging its tail. 'Come 'ere boy' whispered George. The dog happily came to us but wanted to play. It kept barking, so we threw snowballs at it but it thought it was a game and tried to retrieve them.

The red soldiers noticed the commotion and we were quickly captured and put in a compound which was in fact some old tennis courts. We protested and said it would be better for us to pack up and get back to our BMH, but they would not have it. Where the others that were captured were put we had no idea.

We were under guard until an officer marked our cards to indicate we were out of the battle. Our captors were Lancers with some others from a tank regiment. All were well armed. We packed up our gear and drove back to the BMH. Apparently we were the first to be captured that day. We would probably have got away if it had not been for the dog, but it was much warmer back at the BMH.

'Battle Royal' went on for about a week, but we did not have to take any further part. We were issued passes so that if challenged we could show we were exempt.

There were casualties among parachute regiments during their drops. Accidents happened during manoeuvres and also vehicle crashes. There were some fatalities. Tanks ploughed across fields. Compensation of course was given to farmers for damage of crops. I saw a car that had been flattened by a tank when I was going into town for a meal. There were no occupants fortunately. Battle Royal was taken very seriously, except by us National Service laboratory staff.

During this time BMH personnel were investigated by the SIB, the Special Investigation Branch of the army. The army supplied cigarette tickets so that we could buy cigarettes in the NAAFI at a cheap rate. Some soldiers would buy tickets from non-smokers and those that needed the cash. They would then buy cigarettes and sell them outside to German civilians at a profit. Many Catering Corps and Medical Corps soldiers were questioned and several were charged, including a corporal and a sergeant. This meant the 'glasshouse' for them and probable demotion and court martial. It was certainly not worth the risk for a few extra pounds, although I believe they made quite a good living from it while it lasted.

My demob day was getting closer and the lads were talking about the venue for the party. I decided we would all go into town. Our captain wanted to join us, but this was very unusual and normally frowned on. The only time we drank with officers was during rugby matches and the party given by the colonel. We agreed that he could come along, but warned him we would be getting pretty drunk. 'OK' he said. 'The first two rounds will be on me.' 'Right' we said, 'You're on sir.'

The last big booze up we had had was for Moose when he left us to go back to his Canadian unit in Soest. He spent a couple of months' pay on us and I don't think many of us remembered much about it except that he woke up the next morning with a trilby hat and an overcoat that did not belong to him mumbling that he had not had such a good time since Korea. I had a month to go. I was to be demobbed in February, so I had to train one of the staff to take charge of the crystalloid department. Graham, who still had a year to go as he was a regular, was the obvious choice and would be made up to acting corporal. I had no say in the matter, but I would be asked for my comments.

When we were all packing up work, two QARANC nurses turned up in the laboratory asking when my demob party was to take place. Bert had told one of the nurses. Fraternising with them, although frowned upon, was quite the norm.

'Are we invited?' they asked. I was not sure that it was a good idea and told them so. 'Sod you then' said one of the nurses and threw a beaker of water over me. I retaliated with a litre of water from a volumetric flask. Others joined in, including a couple of lance corporals, one of them Graham. There was a lot of noise, laughing and screaming and lots of water.

We had taken for granted that the officers had already left for the officers' mess, but we were wrong. Our major came out of his office in a foul mood. 'You four outside my office first thing after parade and clean up this mess,' he snapped. This was the major I had had trouble with before with the incident of the pump blowing the top off the pressure jars.

Whilst we were cleaning up the water, Q came striding down the corridor. 'When you report for duty in the morning be in your best BD. You know what he's like.'

'Yes Q' I said. 'What were you doing here?'

'I was playing poker in the autoclave room with the German staff and as soon as I heard the major's voice we legged it out through the windows. A good job too, I was losing money. I don't give a shit what you do when off duty. The secret is don't bloody well get caught. I'll see you in the morning sharp.'

We paraded outside the office as ordered and after standing for about ten minutes Q knocked on the door and went in. He immediately came out. 'Right, left turn, quick march. Left right left right halt stand to attention hats off. Defaulters reporting sah.'

'OK Q. Close the door,' ordered the major. He gave us a good dressing down, threatening us with demotion down to private status. This was a worry in that it meant less pay. I decided to interrupt the continuous ticking off the major was giving us. I took a step forward stamping my feet in good drill fashion. 'Sir, permission to speak sir' I shouted. The major stopped his tirade. 'As you were corporal.' growled Q. But I didn't take any notice. 'Sir' I said, 'The cause of the disturbance yesterday evening was mainly my fault. I started it but it snowballed.'

'How did it start corporal, and why were the QARANC nurses in the laboratory?'

I told him and suggested that charges should not be made against the nurses.

'When are you getting demobbed?' he asked.

'In two weeks sir,' I said.

'Right Q, dismiss the others. Corporal, you stay here'.

When the others had been dismissed and marched out he said 'Corporal, I will accept your excuses and take no further action. I have had good reports from your other officers including the colonel and I have been asked to approach you regarding signing on.'

I explained that I had already secured a position in a hospital laboratory in civvy street and thanked him nevertheless. 'OK corporal, dismiss and let's not have any more trouble.'

I put on my beret, saluted and marched out.

Poker was popular in the army, although frowned upon. Gambling for money could get you on a charge, but we used to play some Wednesday evenings. A blanket was thrown over the table and ashtrays were placed beside the seating positions. Beer was brought in from the NAAFI. The cooks usually joined in, bringing their own refreshments. Windows were closed and with the cigarette smoke we created quite an authentic den of iniquity as per American movies.

To make it difficult for us to be caught playing for money we used rubber transfusion bottle washers as 'chips'. They were about the size of a half-crown coin. Black ones were for five pence and red ones for one penny. It became very popular. The money to buy the 'chips' was hidden in a box in Dick's locker and at the end of the game we cashed in the washers. Moose introduced us to several variations of poker. It was dealer's choice and the dealer could call for instance kings and little ones wild, jacks wild, seven card, no peep etc. as well as the usual straight draw and stud.

One evening one of the cooks who had arrived at the BMH only a couple of weeks before was spotted by Dick cheating. He told me during one of the two breaks we took to stretch our legs that when the cook was dealing he was looking at the cards as he dealt them. He had been winning many hands and those he did not win he had folded early. He had also marked some cards with his fingernail. This cheating was only spotted by Dick and not by any of the other players. Dick changed the pack.

'What are we going to do about it?' I said.

'Nae sweat' said Dick. 'I would never cheat because it would spoil the fun of the game, but I'll show ye.'

He had a pack of cards in his hands and I followed him to the latrines. He showed me four aces. 'Put them on top of the pack,' said Dick. I did so and he cut the cards and told me to shuffle them. He then dealt four hands around the wash-basin. Three of the hands were quite high in value, but his hand held four aces. I was impressed.

'This is what we'll do' said Dick. 'When it's my deal I'll deal him a good hand. Yours will be better. We will be playing stud poker. I will stay with you with the betting so that he can either pack or continue. I won't pack. Got the idea?'

I got the idea OK. When it came to Dick's deal he called stud poker. I was given two queens and I asked for three cards. The cook asked for two cards. I realised he probably had three of a kind. When he was dealt his two cards his body language indicated that he had probably been dealt a card giving him four of a kind. I looked at Dick and he gave me a grin. After several rounds of betting four at the table packed. My three cards gave me four queens. He made a bet, not heavy, and I raised the bet. Dick followed with an extra raise and others followed. It started to get a bit heavy with the betting.

After a while the kitty amounted to a few pounds. Apart from the cheating cook the others began to pack, leaving just Dick and me with the cook. The cook raised the bet again confidently. I was beginning to get anxious. After three more rounds of betting Dick packed. I raised the bet again and the cook did likewise. I looked at Dick but got no response. I raised the bet again and this time the cook covered my raise and called me with a smile.

'Two pair' I said. Dick looked puzzled.

'Too bad' said the cook, 'I've got four jacks.' He started to gather in the 'chips'.

'Yes' I said, 'I've got a pair of queens and another pair of queens which means my four queens beat your rotten jacks. Sorry mate!'

The cooks left happily enough except the cheating cook, who left angrily stomping out of the barrack room. He must have lost over a week's pay. 'That will teach the bastard,' said Dick.

When they had gone we celebrated and split the kitty and bought more beer from the NAAFI before they closed and shared it with the boys in the barrack room.

It was February and demob day was looming. I was getting excited. I had written to Queen Mary's Hospital Stratford regarding my position in the laboratory and had been told that although there was not a vacancy I could work at the East Ham Memorial Hospital not far away. That suited me fine. I asked my captain and the colonel and the BMH CO for references. They gladly supplied them and I was very pleased with their reports.

My demob party went well. The captain got drunk and I and the rest of the crew remembered very little about it. The captain however said it was one of the best times he could remember. I do remember he bought most of the beers. He also brought a bottle of whisky from the officers' mess.

The day of demob came. I said goodbye to everyone as they stood together at reception and shook hands with them all, including the colonel and the other officers and Q. The large QARANC nurse was also there with one of the other nurses, and from them much to my surprise I got a kiss. Q drove us to the station, where he shook hands with me again and left. Dick, in civvies, remained behind to see me off. He stayed on the platform until we disappeared from view. We promised to write and see each other in civvy street, and we did. After almost two years working playing and living together during hard and good times the comradeship is fraternal.

My journey to the Hook of Holland was lonely and sad. I was looking forward to life again in civvy street but I missed the lads.

On arrival at Mytchett I met some of the lads I had done my basic training with. Some had not left the country, whilst others were sent all over the world, anywhere where there was a British military presence.

We dumped our gear in a barrack room and immediately retired to the NAAFI. Our feelings regarding Mytchett were different. The corporals and drill sergeants gave me no fears now. We could relax and thumb our noses at them.

The following morning we reported to the Paymaster to collect what was owing to us.

We then had to change into civvies and report with all our gear to a marquee with trestle tables behind which were sergeants and piles of paper work. When my turn came I gave my name, rank and number. The sergeant then started to go through the kit list. In the centre of the marquee there was a huge pile of gear that soldiers before me had discarded. As the sergeant called out the items on his list I threw them on the pile but noted where they landed because I intended to retrieve my boots and backpack. My boots were very comfortable and I did not want to lose them.

When I had completed disposing of some of my kit, I had

to keep some because I was still in the AER (Army Emergency Reserve) for three years. The sergeant said 'One revolver Mark II Belgium with holster and lanyard.' This I have previously mentioned. I was then dismissed and sent to reception to collect my travel documents. Before leaving the marquee I went round the back of the kit mountain and collected my boots and backpack without being noticed. I don't think they were concerned anyway, because I saw other soldiers with retrieved kit.

The journey back home felt strange. It did not really sink in that I was now a civilian again travelling in the back of the army lorry to the station, but it began to become real when I was on the train. My two years was over.

I had three weeks before I started work at the hospital, three weeks with my parents and sweetheart. I spent a few days with friends. My brother was doing his National Service in the Royal Air Force. He was flying in Victor and Vulcan Bombers as a photographer. It took a while to control my language and table manners, but civvy life soon took over.

Back at work, life in the laboratories was not much different, although there was no crystalloid department. The hospital did not have a blood transfusion service.

I was mainly in the bacteriology department and was one of two in the department, which suited me perfectly. I could also concentrate on parasitology and tropical diseases, my main interests. The Royal Army Medical College at Millbank had given me the bug (forgive the pun).

All went well at East Ham Memorial Hospital until the Suez Crisis in October 1956. I had been working in the hospital for just six months when I was ordered via a brown paper OHMS envelope to report the following week back to Mytchett. I told my chief, Tom Lansley, and he said it was quite in order. Nothing could be done. I was to go. He had been a pilot in World War II and a medical laboratory scientific officer, then called a technician, in biochemistry as a profession.

So I received once again my transport documents and orders plus various other papers including pay book and off I went with my kit.

The situation this time was a little different. We did not have to go through basic training. We were trained soldiers. During the three years when you are on AER you have to have fifteen days' training to keep up to scratch, but the Suez crisis negated this.

We were not billeted with the new recruits in huts but in tents, and our beds were canvas X-framed cots. The weather was cold and damp with constant drizzle. We had duckboards on the floor of the tents but only down the centre aisle. To get into bed we would sit on the end of the cot, remove boots and jump back onto the cot and undress. There was always some mud that somehow managed to get into bed with you. At the side of the bed was a small locker, twice cot height, to stow some of our gear. Once in bed however under the blankets, no sheets, smoking a cigarette listening to the rain pattering on the canvas was quite cosy.

I was made up to sergeant. I know not why, but I had to detail the men in the tent, most of them lance corporals and full corporals, to get up at 5 am, finish ablutions by a quarter past and then trudge across the other side of the field we were camped in to light the fires under the stoves for the cooks. There was a line of over a dozen stoves made of brick with iron grids out in the open, and they had to be cleaned out and relit. There was plenty of wood, although damp, but no paper, and the wood was wet. The paper was quite easy to obtain. We ran around the tents and collected the soldiers' newspapers that they had purchased from the NAAFI. With permission, of course!

It was always a very smoky duty because of the wet wood, but we heard no complaints from the cooks. This set-up was for the officers. Who did our stoves and where they were I had no idea. The cookhouse and dining areas were also under canvas.

This life only lasted for about four days and then orders came for us to be kitted out for embarkation to Suez. I didn't think I would ever be involved in a war. We had medical inspections and were issued with kit bags, webbing, spare boots and water bottles, the main armoury of the Medical Corps. The following morning we were transported by lorry to Southampton dock.

We stood on the dockside waiting to go aboard the ships. 'We' included various regiments and corps including the Coldstream Guards. We were there for hours. The parachute regiments and the Marines had already gone and arrived in Suez. After a while we were told to get back in the lorries and to camp. This happened twice. In the middle of the third week we were told to stand down and return our kit. Apparently it was either all over or we were not needed. I do not remember being told much, and one did not rely on army rumours.

The rest of the week was somewhat disorganised and there was not much to do except go to the NAAFI and stroll aimlessly around. Occasionally I met a few of the lads with whom I had done my basic training. Finding out where they had been sent and what they did was a highlight of the latter part of our stay. They had all changed over the two years. I suppose I had too. We were very fit and had matured mentally too.

Once again we had to put our gear back onto the growing mountain of army equipment. I managed another pair of boots for my father and another backpack.

Although still on the AER list, I was not bothered by the Ministry of Defence again. I settled down to civilian life, but I never forgot how to salute or march and as previously mentioned I never forgot my army number.

Basic training was a hard, frightening and lonely experience, but after those three months I would never have missed the rest of the time, and perhaps the hard work and discipline helped one to appreciate it. The comradeship in the army was paramount.

It taught me to understand people from one end of the United Kingdom to the other, so for those like myself visiting other countries, it was also a very good educational experience.

Security was another aspect of army life. Everything was done for you. You felt secure, but as an NCO you had a lot of responsibility because rules and regulations must not be broken. If they were, you were punished. This was also good for one's character. Humility was something you learnt to handle from the beginning. This was another character-building exercise which is not fully understood by individuals outside the services. I worked and played hard and gave I hope as much as I received from the experience.

The word 'humility' should read thus in the dictionary: 'not looking a drill corporal in the eye whilst he is shouting verbal abuse at you nose to nose and you are breathing in his halitosis, while trying not even to raise an eyebrow or you will be charged for dumb insolence'. That's humility, but I recommend the National Service experience to all eighteen-year-olds.

From here on I am known.

Postscript

By Joy Eldridge

On leaving National Service Brian resumed his career at East Ham Memorial Hospital, moving on to Connaught Hospital, then Wanstead Hospital. He passed his basic Medical Technology exams and then specialised in Bacteriology and finally in Parasitology and Mycology, obtaining the Fellowship of the Institute of Medical Technology, an equivalent to today's MSC in Biomedical Sciences. In the early seventies he took up the post of Chief of Bacteriology at Whipps Cross Hospital. His passion for parasitology made him an excellent teacher when he lectured on the subject to young medical students. He remained at Whipps until he retired.

Shortly after leaving National Service he married his childhood sweetheart Olwen, and he soon became a father to Bronwen who later gave him his first grandchild, Ruby. Sadly, this marriage was not successful.

He met his soulmate, Joy, at Wanstead Hospital. They married and he became a father for the second time, to Gemma, and later grandfather to Ethan and Summer.

Brian's three grandchildren doted on their Poppa. He enthralled them with stories from his wartime memories and enthused them with his knowledge of the natural world.

On his eightieth birthday he returned to Münster to seek out some of his old haunts, which held happy memories. An old menu led him to the Altes Gasthaus Leve. There he remembered where he had sat when a young waitress had cut up his food for him due to his heavily bandaged hand. Amazingly that young waitress turned out to be the present owner's grandmother. The owners were very happy to see their menu from the fifties, and he came away with a memento in the form of a jug.

Brian's fascination with nature was translated into many beautiful landscape, bird and animal paintings. His last painting was completed in just one day, immediately before he was admitted into hospital. He died there just a week later, on March 29th 2020.